FIGURES OF MANKIND

Where Are We
RUNNING?

P.Y. Rollin

ISBN 978-2-9701241-0-8
ISBN 978-2-9701241-1-5 (ebook)

Bridge⌣Books

Chemin du Bochet 32
CH-1025 St-Sulpice
Switzerland

www.bridge-books.com

contact@bridge-books.com

FOREWORD

After a Master of Science degree in information technologies, business and manufacturing, and a sixteen month detour on mandatory military duty in the French Navy, I worked for two decades as a consultant on large IT projects for global corporations (ERP implementations). These very complex projects consisted of implementing all business processes of a group, from finance and purchasing to sales and manufacturing, worldwide over all the subsidiaries. This required listening to top management to understand their vision and to elaborate the future business model of their company. Subsequently, we worked closely with people from the field to understand their day-to-day constraints, and to have them regularly validate the relevancy of the solutions that we were implementing. Such an approach was essential to the success of the project, because the actual knowledge of the reality of the business was at field level, not at top management's.

Many of the choices made during implementation were key

options in a very sophisticated database. However, what mattered was to ensure that the business people were the decision owners. So our consultants' key competence was to make it simple, to present complex choices in a manner easy to understand, and to let the people from the field decide.

I was good at recruiting excellent consultants (I am very proud of my past teams) and at making complexity look simple. But the real talent of a consultant stretched beyond this. The magic was to make people smart. We called this approach, "Make the client be the hero". It was not just a marketing or management trick. Most of our clients' key contributors were not top decision makers; they were normal people usually asked to deliver the job and to comply with the instructions. From time to time they were invited to continuous improvement workshops, but that's it. Yet, during our projects, they were asked to take hundreds of decisions: some on small options, and some on major choices for the group. This was because top management alone could not handle the complexity of such huge projects. So for a year or two, the people from the field were empowered as the strategic day-to-day decision makers in order to elaborate the future business processes of their company. And guess what. That's exactly how the right choices were made. Because normal people working together and rightly empowered turn out to be incredibly smart.

And that's what I have tried to do with this book: explain our complex global situation in simple terms; empower normal people, a category in which we all fit as citizens of the world; and ignite a spark of wisdom that will enlighten our future. For this, I had to review some of the bad news that we are served daily. This might sound callous as you read along, and I sincerely apologize in advance to anyone who was personally impacted by one of the dramas that I mention. My words cannot be anything but awkward and inappropriate to anyone who lost a loved one in these events. But it is important for us not to be overwhelmed with the bad news that feeds rampant pessimism. I am well aware that casualties are not "numbers" but real people with relatives and friends who miss them deeply. Yet rationality helps us to better apprehend situations and to think over the big picture.

Flourishing political populism illustrates how so many of us are lost in fears about complex globalization. I consider that such anxieties are legitimate, even though I disagree with how they are being exploited. There are scary questions to be addressed when it comes to globalization, and more distressingly, there are hundreds of small or major choices to be made, right now.

So in this book, I have tried to do my usual job. I worked to make it simple, and to make us smart at understanding what is going on. I have tried to enable each of us to become a strategic day-to-day decision maker.

Globalization is being managed in a top-down approach by the United Nations, the World Economic Forum, political elites, CEOs, and many brilliant people who issue many brilliant statements. But normal people do not really buy it, right? So shouldn't we try to run this game the other way round, with a "bottom-up" managerial approach?

Each of us has a unique contribution to make in this global future that we are building altogether, unconsciously yet undeniably.

My little talent now is to tell a story. Yours will be to make it happen.

Finally, this little book is about how to write a larger book that we are all authors of, right now:

The Book of Mankind.

CONTENTS

INTRODUCTION

It all started with an earthquake.

Earthquakes are strange. Suddenly, without warning, everything starts to shake. You have no idea what is going on, and a few seconds later countless people are trapped. Dozens of neighbors, friends and family members are hurt, dead, or missing. Fortunately, catastrophic earthquakes occur very rarely. Yet, think of a forty kilometers drive (or about twenty-five miles): that is the distance from your home straight down to the fiery 1,000 °C upper mantle*. So thin indeed is the Earth's crust on which we all live.

Every day, about 1,400 earthquakes occur around the world. Most are very small, yet about twenty percent of them are *felt*[1]. Such a sensation is imprecise, though. While a medium earthquake might not be perceived, some small ones are noticeable. This is why, in 1935, the scientist Charles Richter introduced a scale that measures

_____

* 1,800 °F

an earthquake's magnitude, from one to nine. This is what figures are for. They help us to compare, to assess and to better understand our world.

Events reported by the media, however, are rarely placed on any kind of scale. What matters for the newscaster is how to generate an audience, which will then watch the commercials that follow. Therefore, news focuses on inspiring an emotion, using storytelling methods with striking images and heart-broken witnesses. This produces an emotional roller coaster of tragic information, later balanced by comedy shows or action movies, and punctuated with ads. As viewers, we cannot escape being flung around in repetitive loops of pessimism, fun, and indifference. How can we avoid becoming disillusioned? How can we get off such a dizzying merry-go-round?

In order to better manage the news we are given, we need to measure, compare, and study a little. Like seismologists with earthquakes, we need to find the figures that are appropriate to measure our world.

Figures provide us with an accurate outlook on reality. They help us to literally *figure things out*. They allow us to understand trends, and to foresee our future. They might even offer us a nice surprise.

If we were to take off the grey pessimistic glasses we have been prescribed, and gaze at the world with fresh eyes, then *what would we see?*

Let us take a look.

Part I

Dancing with the News

In order to better understand this world, we first need to sort through the bad news. Let's dive into a few case studies.

AN EARTHQUAKE ON MY PLATE

D O YOU RECALL where you were on the evening of January 13th, 2010? I was in my kitchen, preparing a quick dinner, after an ordinary day at work. I heated up a snack I'd bought nearby. I sat at my table and turned on the TV. A news flash appeared, announcing an earthquake that had happened just a few hours earlier in Haiti. The report seemed hastily patched together, but to my surprise, feedback was already streaming in directly from the field. Interviews were being conducted with people on the scene, who repeated how terrible, terrible, terrible it was. Pictures were displayed of severely damaged buildings, including a local cathedral, the presidential palace; and many other buildings. One video tracked through the streets past people lying on the ground, or weeping inconsolably. Another showed a man trying to pull his child out of the rubble, then zoomed in for a close-up of an anonymous, lifeless body. The Haitian Prime Minister, Jean-Max Bellerive, mentioned an estimated 100,000 casualties[2]. After all of this awful news, the newscaster reported on the international rescue effort arriving in the area: three planes, two hundred firemen, a dozen rescue dogs to investigate the rubble. Right after that came the usual commercials.

I turned off my TV, but my mind wouldn't let go of the image of that dead body. I looked at my plate, and threw the hamburger away. I stared at my French fries. One hundred thousand casualties. What did that mean? Inadvertently, I started counting: I had about fifty fries on my plate. If they were buildings, that meant *two thousand people trapped under each fry*. Even if ten percent of them were still alive, how could a rescue of so many be achieved? Could two hundred firemen really handle such a situation? How many hidden survivors would twelve dogs be able to retrieve from the rubble? The situation seemed to be so hopelessly under-evaluated. Then a dreadful thought struck me: "Most of the people currently buried alive will die in the next 48 hours." It was impossible to save them all. Perhaps one percent could be rescued[*]...

---

[*] Eventually an estimated 132 survivors were saved from beneath collapsed buildings.

Then I looked at my watch. I was running late for a drink with some friends. Time to move on.

*   *   *

Around some beers that night in a pub playing jazz music, my friends and I had our usual chitchat. Girlfriends, boyfriends, bosses, colleagues, new projects, deadlines to be met, vacations to plan. One mentioned the disaster: "Did you hear about the tragic earthquake that happened today in Haiti?" We all sympathized for a minute. Then we switched back to chatting about football games. What else could we do?

Back home, I checked the news again. The TV presenter had a five-minute detailed report on four adults and three children being saved from under collapsed buildings. Great, I thought, sure, but it seemed like a drop in the ocean given the total number of fatalities. An international organization had allocated hydraulic engineers and experts in sanitation to ensure access to safe water and toilet facilities, and avoid a second tragedy from subsequent epidemics. Their foresight sounded like a better strategic move to me. The estimated death toll had already increased to 150,000 people.

I realized that I was missing a scale of sorts to better understand this situation. What could I compare this with? Suddenly an image popped into my mind: the atomic bomb. How many casualties had the Hiroshima or Nagasaki atomic bombings caused? Such figures abound on the Internet, but vary greatly, depending on how they are quantified: are we talking about immediate deaths, or those who passed away shortly after the events, or those who would die later from radiation-related cancers? I settled on an approximated number of deaths directly related to the bombings, either immediate or temporally close. For Hiroshima it was 75,000, and for Nagasaki 50,000.

I was dumbstruck. Imagine dropping an atomic bomb onto the capital of one of the poorest countries in the world, then having the plane turn on its wing and fire a second one right after. Such was the impact of the Haiti earthquake. It was more devastating than the Hiroshima and Nagasaki bombings combined.

*   *   *

An acquaintance of mine worked in international military logistics. I knew he would likely be involved in some operations following the catastrophe in Haiti, so I sent him a short email, pointing out the magnitude of the event. I mentioned this atomic bomb comparison. Two months later he thanked me, acknowledging the usefulness of my analogy. Such was my very small contribution to this drama.

Back to January 12th. That night I remembered the "World Trade Center" movie by Oliver Stone, where survivors manage to escape from the rubble. I was not in New York on 9/11/2001, but some friends of mine were. Like any New Yorkers, they all knew someone directly affected by the tragedy.

I thought of these children who had buried their parents in empty coffins, because most of the bodies could not be retrieved. Coincidently, I had attended my own dad's burial the week before. When a tragedy touches you personally, you do not care about what's happening in the rest of the world. At the same time, though, you empathize, and somehow connect, with others affected by similar cruel twists of fate.

I realize how close to the line of decency I am when I make the equations that follow. I understand how shocking this might seem to many people, because tragedies are not meant to be described in such clinical terms. But in order to accurately measure the scale of the Haitian earthquake, one must realize that we are talking of fifty times the magnitude of the 9/11 tragedy. Instead of four planes that killed innocent people, the deaths in Haiti would equate to two hundred planes. It's the equivalent to a terrorist attack that would go on for two full days, non-stop including overnight, instead of one hour. Such magnitude is staggering. How can one even contemplate managing the respectful burials of 150,000 people?

*   *   *

Like most people, I wished I could do a little something for Haiti. I thought of this country, every now and then. I kept up with the news, and tried to be a tiny part of this public opinion that provokes government actions and encourages humanitarian funding. I hoped it might bring some help to those afflicted by the tragedy.

Somehow our thoughts had an impact. The catastrophe in Haiti generated massive global mobilization, in terms of private donations, government support, and personal initiatives by celebrities. Mid-term plans were laid, and many international organizations got involved. Solidarity worked, at least initially. Billions of dollars were provided in aid: enough, in theory, to spawn an economic miracle in this small and desperately poor country. Yet, five years later, forty percent of the population still lacked access to proper water and sanitation[3]. The island has since been exposed to severe epidemics, including a cholera outbreak that was sadly due to foreign UN soldiers. Today, some judge the international effort for this earthquake to have been a fiasco[4]. What went wrong? We do not know.

When was the last time you heard anything about Haiti? What I find amazing is that this earthquake was on the air for a few weeks or months at most. Once a year, some media channels recall it. Other than that, it has quickly slipped from the public's consciousness.

And that is the most unsettling lesson to be drawn from such stories. Not only do the newscasters jump from one event to another, but they don't put any of them into perspective. In fact, they do their best not to. In the same tragic tone, they announce an earthquake of 150,000 fatalities, a three percent stock market fall, the suicide of a popular movie actor, or a train accident that caused two hundred casualties on the other side of the world. The purpose of this game is to grab your attention with storytelling techniques and endless content, and hold you captive for ongoing advertising. Can we believe that this is still how the news works in the twenty-first century?

How can we take a step back from such events? How can we handle such dramas psychologically, when they are literally thrown in our faces every night? How can we teach our children to deal with them, if we, as adults, are not able to evaluate a situation and reflect?

Let's bring a few figures into play and reconsider a few major events of the past decade. Figures enable us to take power over how information is presented by the media.

CHAPTER 2

FIGURES OF LIBERTY

W HICH GLOBAL EVENTS have impacted you over the last decade? You might first think of Fukushima, and the Asian tsunami. You might also have been struck by the significant flooding in India some years ago. Today, you might point to the Syrian civil war as an ongoing disaster. Yet do we have any idea of how all these events might compare to each other on a global scale? Perhaps the suicide of Robin Williams, a charismatic actor whose films we have loved, touches us as deeply as a tsunami on the other side of the world. Is the death of one famous American actor as weighty an event as a catastrophe that results in the deaths of thousands? One may argue that tragedies are not meant to be compared. But if we cannot "measure" the bad news properly, then how can we rebalance it with the good news? For there is indeed some good news, which we will investigate later in this book. Nevertheless, in order to be optimistic and not simply naive, we must face the reality of our world, and learn how to assess the bad news with which we are overwhelmed.

The spectacular incident at the Fukushima nuclear plant in 2011 happened in a very developed and densely populated country. It resulted in 1,600 fatalities[*][5]. While obviously devastating to those involved, this is a relatively small number compared to what happened in Haiti. The Indian flood in September 2014 had damaging impacts on 400,000 people. In the end, though, less than 500 died[6]. The Asian tsunami on December 2004 amounted to a death toll of 230,000[7]. These are three figures that relate to three very different magnitudes, for three events that were presented to us very similarly as "tragedies". But the first two may be considered "little" catastrophes once they are compared to the Asian tsunami and the Haitian earthquake. Using our previous "atomic bomb scale", where one atomic bomb equates roughly to 60,000 deaths[**], then in terms of death toll the Indian flood converts to 0.008, Fukushima to 0.027, Haiti to 3.3 and the Asian tsunami to 4 atomic bombs. Haiti's earthquake, indeed, eventually amounted to a death toll of 200,000.

---

[*] Most of these fatalities were indirect consequences, due not to the nuclear effects but to the ensuing evacuation of the area. The Tohoku earthquake and tsunami that damaged the nuclear plant had a death toll of 16,000 fatalities, but 90% of them were not related to the accident at Fukushima.

[**] "The atomic bomb", here and further on, refers to the historical ones used in Nagasaki and Hiroshima.

The Syrian civil war is still going on as I write this book. Are we aware of the figures regarding Syria? In such scattered and complex conflict it is difficult to gather facts or numbers, but estimates average at least 300,000 deaths between 2011 and 2016[8]. This is higher than all events previously mentioned. We are now talking of the equivalent of five atomic bombs cast on one country, with minimal action from international peacekeeping forces. An award for the best actor in a non-supporting role could be granted to the United Nations for this one! Some even talk of about two million casualties, wounded or dead. This figure represents ten percent of the Syrian population of twenty-one million before war. An estimated four million have escaped from the country. Most Western political leaders appear more annoyed with the consequences for their own countries of such a refugee crisis, than with the humanitarian catastrophe it represents.

I shall not comment any further on Syria, as it is a complex piece of political theater that I would not pretend to understand fully. And yet…

*   *   *

By the way, any ideas on Haiti's total population? It stands at ten million. So the earthquake that struck that small country killed 2% of its population. Let's call this the "fatality rate". This is a rather cynical yet meaningful calculation, as it enables us to qualify the "peak effect". Allow me to elaborate on this with a basic example. If one parent of a family were to die in an accident, it is obvious that this would have a shattering effect on the children. But if both parents were to die together, then this would be more devastating than twice the previous tragedy, because of the logistical and practical consequences. Who, for example, is going to take care of the children? This "peak effect" works similarly in large disasters: if a catastrophe hits a large number of people, but this number remains low relative to the total population (of the city, country, etc.), then many people and local infrastructures are available to handle the situation: hospitals, facilities, law enforcement, public administrations, schools, private companies to keep the economy rolling, etcetera. The higher the peak, the greater the repercussions of the tragedy.

This is why the aftermath of the Asian tsunami was easier to handle than the Haitian earthquake. The former had a higher death toll than the latter, but a much lower fatality rate of 0.017%*. International aid was effective, as local infrastructures could be relied on, and thus the regions recovered quickly. A 2% fatality rate, such as that of the Haitian earthquake, means a "high peak" catastrophe which is much more difficult to address.

What about 9/11? Of course, using calculations seems insensitive here, as we are comparing two different

---

* Cumulated population of the four countries most impacted by the Asian Tsunami: 1,400 million people ((Indonesia, Sri Lanka, India, Thailand).

realities. The earthquake and the tsunami were natural disasters, whereas 9/11 was a deliberate attack, an act of mass murder. Terrorists aim to spread terror, so it is legitimate that such events incite an emotional response that is proportionally much higher that other tragedies. And yet, the best answer to terror is to hold it back, and to resist falling into the emotional trap of fear and hatred. Some figures are tough to work with, and it is important to keep in mind that every catastrophe is heartbreaking for those it impacts. But accurate assessment helps us to better understand a situation and make good decisions.

In total, 9/11 amounted to 2,977 fatalities[9]. Ninety percent of them occurred in New York City. Calculating the fatality rate is awkward and somehow imprecise, as it depends on the geographic zone you consider. With NYC's population at eight million people, this would translate to a 0.037% fatality rate, two times higher than the Asian tsunami rate. But Haiti's 2% is still fifty-four times higher. Let us zoom in on the dedication of the NY firemen, who walked into the burning towers without hesitation: 343 lost their lives, out of a total of 8,648 firemen[10]. This equates to a 4% fatality rate, twice that of the Haitian earthquake. This illustrates what a high price the NY firemen and firewomen paid for helping those trapped inside the buildings. We already knew this. We do remember.

When it comes to assessing 9/11, shouldn't the US and Allied soldiers killed while fighting in Afghanistan and

Iraq be considered as ensuing casualties? How many of these "Liberty soldiers" died?

We are talking of 3,547 deaths of coalition soldiers in Afghanistan (one-third of whom were non-American), and 4,852 deaths of coalition soldiers in Iraq (one-fifteenth of whom were non-American)[11].

As a first comment, this translates to more than 1,450 non-American soldiers who died fighting for the United States as a consequence of the 9/11 attack. Was this mentioned at any time during the last US presidential campaigns as an acknowledgement to US Allies? For each victim of 9/11, roughly three coalition soldiers (Americans and Allies) were killed fighting back. Do we remember a single one of their names? Did anyone notice that eighty-nine of them were French soldiers, killed in Afghanistan while some American citizens were bashing them[12]? Eighty-nine is more than the number of fries in a plate...

*　　*　　*

What does it take to become a soldier deployed to Afghanistan or Iraq? For a while, you may have thought about joining the army. Perhaps the notion of belonging to a country, a vague idea of patriotism, made its way to the forefront of your mind. But to become willing to fight and kill... this question takes a little longer to answer.

It took me twelve years to make such a choice. Since I was

a child, I had been aware that if I were to agree to do my military service, then "mandatory" in France*, it meant I was potentially accepting, one day, to kill someone under order. I had surgery to correct my shortsightedness so that I could join the Navy as an officer on watch, an opportunity offered to graduated engineers. Then I realized that I was flying away from the question that had puzzled me for a decade. I decided to address it properly. If it had to be done, I would do it. I decided that I would kill, with no hate, in lucidity, as professionally as a surgeon if ordered to do so by my country. So, I called the Navy central office and had my request modified, in order to join the Marine Commandos – the French equivalent to the US Navy Seals. I prepared myself for six months, was admitted, and trained in the army for eight weeks. That meant running with a fifteen-kilo load over distances I had never run before, diving in freezing water, completing assault courses and night trainings, and shooting with a variety of weapons. I signed this particular form, which meant I was committing to do whatever mission was required, wherever. I was selected for the seven week intense commando training. This was already an achievement. Once in, I ran a jungle assault course under heavy rain, grabbing at wet slippery ropes ten meters off the ground. I ran a commando assault course, in the middle of which I jumped from a four meter high platform. I confess I screamed upon landing. I had badly twisted my

---

* Alternative civil duty options were available.

knee. End of the story. Cross-ligament, edge ligament, cartilages all suffered damage. I was awarded an eleven month medical treat for two days of Special Forces training. My very first night at the hospital, I watched the TV news: some French soldiers were coming back from their tour of duty in Yugoslavia, with tired eyes. Their lieutenant summed up their story: "At our level, we did what we could." I realized that so had I. Even though I would never wear the green beret I had been training for, for a short time I had joined that club of people who "run for the others". But within a minute, I had been moved to another club, the club of those who cannot walk nor even go to the toilet without help. No doctor would promise me then that I could ever walk again without a stick.

Was it worth it? While recovering from my knee injury, I had time think about that question. I watched the news, listened to the mood of the people and, once I returned to the normal world, the one I was ready to fight for, I understood that no one really cared about that kind of commitment. Yet, surprisingly the answer made its way in my mind: yes. Even knowing where this would lead me, I think I would do it again. I was strong, so it was my turn to go. Defend the less strong. Defend the defenseless. Some would call it duty, but over there people just considered it quite normal. And I liked it that way.

From time to time though, I admit I have a little inner laugh when listening to political speeches, or reading corporations' websites: "Our values, bla bla bla." No one bragged like that in the training camp.

* * *

Don't we owe the US and Allied soldiers some honesty about an embarrassing question? When it comes to Iraq, was such a war legitimate? Was it strategically relevant? At the level of each individual soldier, it is a most noble and respectful choice to respond to the call of duty. At the level of decision-makers, was it the right choice to send them to war over there? There were almost twice as many US soldiers sacrificed in Iraq compared to Afghanistan. Who is responsible for the deaths of 4,530 US soldiers and 322 coalition soldiers in Iraq?

And what about all the so-called collateral damage? About 100,000 civilians died during the 2003-2011 Iraq war[13]; this is about thirty times the number of people who lost their lives on 9/11.

The fatality rate of civilians dead in Iraq is apparently a medium one: 0.36%*. Embarrassingly, here this means that such a high number of civilian victims was somehow *predictable*. Yet, was this information put on the table when the reasons for the Iraq war were explained to us, citizens of the world? Has anyone ever communicated such figures to us since then?

---

* Iraq population (2003-11): 28 million people.

A decade later, we know that Saddam Hussein did not have weapons of mass destruction, nor any connection to Al Qaeda or Osama bin Laden. He had no plan to threaten the United States. Consequently, the undeniable answer is, "No, it was not the right choice to send American and Allied soldiers to Iraq."

So who is responsible for this decision? To whom should we send the bill for the deaths of 4,852 coalition soldiers and 100,000 civilians?

CHAPTER 3

DEMOCRACY AND THE KINGMAKERS

WAS THE 2003-2011 Iraq war a mistake? Unfortunately, yes. This question has been asked frequently during years, and quite consistently answered. Who is responsible for it? Who is accountable for the loss of so many human lives?

President George W. Bush decided to go to war. The American Congress voted for it. The United Nations never explicitly approved nor rejected it, because the French Foreign Affairs minister had made it clear that if a vote were to be officially requested, France would use its power to veto. He just forgot to remind the US that your best friend is not so much the one who follows you wherever, but rather the one who tells you loud and clear when you are taking the wrong path. France predicted exactly what sadly happened. It was a war that the US would win, but without strong international legitimacy upfront, they would not be able to secure peace afterwards. And with no evidence provided of the presence of weapons of mass destruction in Iraq, the legitimacy to attack the country was nonexistent. Furthermore, where did this strange idea of invasion come from? Wouldn't a series of strikes on key military compounds have been more relevant?

So, finally, the right question is: who put the main decision taker, Mr. Bush, in place? Let us rewind the history tape a few years…

On February 8th 2004 in Tennessee, as reported by the *New York Times*, Al Gore severely criticized Bush for his decision to invade Iraq[14]:

> "President Bush betrayed this country! He played on our fears. He took America on an ill-conceived foreign adventure dangerous to our troops, an adventure preordained and planned before 9/11 ever took place."

Further back, on September 23rd 2002 in San Francisco, a few weeks before the US Congress authorized the use of military force against Iraq, Gore made a detailed speech questioning the Bush administration's strategy and stating that such a vote would "dim the American principle"[15]. It is fair to say that if Gore had been elected president instead of Bush Jr, the decision-making process would have been much more solid. Most likely, history would have followed a different course and the turmoil of the Iraq war would not have happened. Trillions of dollars would have been saved for the American budget. There would have been no room for ISIS to develop... It would have been a better call, no?

Let us rewind two more years. Do you remember the official final margin of vote by which Bush won the swing state of Florida against Al Gore[16]?

That was 537.

*　　*　　*

If 537 people had voted for Gore instead of Bush, the course of history would have changed, and most likely, the 4,530 American soldiers, 322 Allied soldiers and 100,000 Iraqi civilians would still be alive. This means that each vote weighed the same as the lives of eight American soldiers, 0.6 Allied soldier, and two hundred Iraqi civilians. That's a lot of names to be written down on each ballot, is it not? Who among the Bush voters in Florida could have been aware of the overwhelming responsibility they held in their hands?

Should we keep this story in mind the next time we vote? In truth, the math is even more severe. To change the result of the election, we needed only a single vote margin. Hence if only half of that number had voted Gore instead of Bush, then Gore would have won. Only 269 voters made Bush president. Let me introduce you properly to these 269 individuals: they are the kingmakers.

Imagine a Congress of a hundred members, where forty-nine are from the left, forty-nine from the right, and two are from an independent party. Who runs the country then? The two representatives from the tiny party do. Whatever the law is being discussed, these folks hold the keys to pass it or reject it. They are the two kingmakers among a 100-member assembly.

Now, when it comes to a presidential election, does it work so differently? The Bush versus Gore US presidential election was unusual due to such a narrow margin in Florida, and due to the Electoral College mechanism. Nevertheless, what is the margin for most elections within our Western democracies? Most of the time, we are talking of one or two percent. A large victory would be a four to six percent margin. Divided by two, this translates to a tiny percentage of key voters, let us say one percent on average. Due to abstention, only fifty to eighty percent of the eligible population actually votes. This means that only 0.7% of the electors trigger the final result. Moreover, children and teenagers are not entitled to vote so, relative to the whole population, this percentage is even smaller. In our free world, about 0.5% of the citizens are "kingmakers". Are you one of them?

The question is not so much whether you vote blue or

red, left or right. Despite the previous case, the matter is not to point a finger at who voted for Bush or Gore in Florida. The real issue is: *how* did one vote? Think of last time you voted. Did you run through the pros and cons? Analyze your decision on a sheet of paper? Were you aware of the stakes? Did you follow your instincts? Did you make a last minute choice, leaving it to chance? Or did you stay at home, disinterested in politics?

Most people have their minds made up before a campaign, regardless of how it runs. They are the fixed positions. Others follow whatever trend arises from advertisements, newspapers, and influencers. These will usually be split equally, as old political dogs from both sides know the tricks to influence them. The last category of voters is a small number: those who will consider all options, carefully weigh each one, and thoughtfully make a decision. These are the ones who believe that their individual vote can really make a difference. They are the kingmakers.

This is how democracy works. Once aware of this, make your vote count. Become a kingmaker.

*   *   *

Every so often, we head to the voting booths and cast a ballot. Then what? We work. We buy products. Follow the news. Play sports. Watch movies. Share drinks. Make love. Yet, we are scrutinized. Our likes on social networks, our clicks on webpages, our online search habits, our physical itineraries: all our behaviors are gathered, big-data-processed and modeled into patterns to more efficiently sell us products and services. Is this situation a massive manipulation of the many by the few? Perhaps. But what if trends work similarly to votes? What if it takes a tiny minority to push the ball and get it rolling down one side of the hill versus the other? How could we have an impact on the whole game?

This has already been going on for decades with TV advertising. Until recently, the options for the targeted consumer were simply whether to buy brand A or brand B. But now, with the Internet, we can share information, comment on it, and react instantly. Competition has never been more intense. The Internet user is much more powerful than the twentieth century consumer. And real power arises when a sum of tiny choices becomes a trending topic.

We are like the pixels of a digital image. Alone, we have no effect. Together, we are more than the sum of all individuals. The image is more than a total of pixels. From an assembly of tiny elements can surge a powerful picture. Likewise, each of us is part of this "public opinion" that commands world leaders.

How is public opinion typically formed? By influencers, such as journalists, political leaders, and fashion editors? Mostly, and the outcome is messy. So, how can we take the lead? How do we become kingmakers?

Stop being manipulated. Dig deeper beyond the news, and seek out all the *other* information available. Analyze, compare, and contrast. Figure it out!

This would be a good start. We can do better.

CHAPTER 4

INFOTAINMENT

I UNDERSTAND THE STAKE of being part of this public opinion. Like pixels in a digital image, or like the dots of a pointillism painting, each of us participates in the global picture. Yet, what can I do? How can I *willingly* contribute to the whole? How can I cultivate my "citizen consciousness"?

In other words: what have I missed?

In the twenty-first century, with the exception of the ongoing civil war in Syria, natural disasters seem to be more tragic than wars. The Haitian earthquake (2008) and the Asian tsunami (2004) resulted in a higher death toll than the war in Iraq (2003-11) and the war in Afghanistan (2001-14). Is it always this way?

Is public opinion strong enough to influence diplomatic actions and prevent wars?

Let us take a step further back, to the previous decade: the 1990s.

In a nutshell, it started beautifully. When Saddam Hussein abruptly invaded Kuwait, the United Nations stood up and, for once, actually "united". George *H.W.* Bush (senior) carefully built a legitimate multi-country military coalition, unanimously granted to enforce international law and liberate Kuwait. Led by the United States, such a coalition crushed the Iraqi army. Let us not forget that Iraq's army was, at the time, considered to be the fourth most powerful army in the world!

A new chapter in the history of the world had just been written. Dictators and villains were confined to the past or, at least, contained in their own country. Yippee!

And then oops, we tripped over the carpet. That was Yugoslavia.

*   *   *

Let's admit that Yugoslavia was a more complex story to understand than the aggressive invasion of Kuwait by Saddam Hussein, without any oil buried nearby. This former country of twenty-three million people, in which the First World War began (Sarajevo, June 1914), communist yet officially non-aligned, was a patchwork combining six states, four languages, three religions and two alphabets. This federation was contained under the Tito dictatorship for three decades, before drifting apart after his death in 1980. It deteriorated into a civil war with the arrival of Slobodan Milosevic as head of the Serbian Republic, thanks to his delusional dream of restoring a "Great Serbia" - a fairly common philosophy among such leaders, apparently.

It took a full decade for the UN to restore order and send Milosevic before an international court on charges of mass murder, along with another dangerous local leader, Radovan Karadzic. This was a brilliant demonstration of how inefficient and ridiculous the UN can sometimes be. Would you believe that, even facing a deliberate aggression, the UN peacekeeping soldiers were initially not allowed to have any bullets in their weapons? Later, they had the right to shoot back only if personally attacked. In full contradiction of this supposed world-standard right of legitimate defense (which technically applies to oneself, but also to the defenseless nearby), the peacekeepers were not allowed to defend the children being killed before their eyes in the streets of Sarajevo, by snipers hidden in the surrounding mountains. They were forbidden to even attempt to fire back.

It took 3.5 years for the UN to decide to bomb the surrounding mountains of Sarajevo using NATO fighter jets, and promptly put an end to the siege of the city from Serbian snipers, artillery and tanks. In the meantime, 5,000 civilians had been killed[17].

In fairness to the UN, the start of the conflict was confusing.

What was the trick? Milosevic was cheating and, like all cheaters, was very good at hiding it. How? Local antagonists from a Serbian minority in Croatia were stirring up trouble in Krajina, a region close to the Serbian border. The Croatian police went to arrest the troublemakers, who did not comply and complained that they were being harassed by Croatian police. Then Milosevic, the Serbian president, turned the story upside down by claiming that the Serbian minority in Croatia had to be protected. He conveniently invaded Krajina, officially to restore peace and order in this region, which would subsequently become part of Serbia, of course. His game was identified and pinpointed as early as 1992 by Western experts on Yugoslavian politics, such as Paul Garde in a book thoroughly explaining how the conflict started and how it would evolve[18].

Media coverage was very imprecise. What most influenced public opinion was likely the Srebrenica Massacre (8,000 civilian deaths)[19]. Do we have any idea of the *total* number of fatalities from the Yugoslavia civil war[20]? It was 140,000. This equates to 2.3 atomic bombs...

Who is responsible for such a fiasco? Apparently, no one. That is the beauty of our democracies, when they start playing games within the United Nations.

*   *   *

Meanwhile, somewhere else in the world, in 1994, a million people were killed within a few months. One million... Did you ever hear of that story? No? Was it ignored because of where it was taking place, Africa?

But we do care about Africa! Let us recall this "USA for Africa" fundraising song, in the 80s: a durable number one hit on the charts. It was one of the best successes ever for a single with twenty million copies sold! Remember Lionel Ritchie, Stevie Wonder, Paul Simon, Michael Jackson, Tina Turner, Bruce Springsteen, and so many charismatic voices, singing together "*We Are The World*".

And yet, nine years later, in 1994, a human-caused tragedy generated a million fatalities in three months[21]. The equivalent of five Haitian earthquakes or seventeen atomic bombs.

The story emerged thanks to another song, written by a Belgian singer. It was also quite popular: a top hit for ten weeks in twelve different countries. It soared to number twenty-five on the US charts. One million copies of the song were sold - one million - and five-hundred million people watched the clip online.

"Papaoutai" is a light pop song with a catchy rhythm, which you have most likely heard on the radio.

Stromae admits he wrote it with the ink of his tears. Papaoutai literally translates as "daddy-where-are-you". Stromae's father was killed in the Rwandan genocide, in 1994. At that time Stromae was nine years old, which means that, ironically, he was born the year when "*We Are the World*" was recorded.

Where is Rwanda?

* * *

Let's not get distracted by blaming the UN and the media, or by searching for other excuses. We are served the information that we want, right?

Is it shocking that no peacekeeping forces were sent to Rwanda even though a conflict was already being handled in Yugoslavia? Absolutely. That makes two fiascos and no excuse for the UN and all related decision-makers. No excuse for our heads of state. No excuse, finally, for our public opinion. Us!

How were we not made aware of this genocide? Was it not tragic enough? We are talking of a seventy percent fatality rate. Almost fifty times the earthquake peak effect...

Why were we so poorly informed about Rwanda?

I do not know.

Most likely, traditional media was just not able to build a decent story out of it, one that would be solid enough to catch our attention. And sell.

In our over-mediatized world, with hundreds of TV channels, radio stations, newspapers and now internet media competing to provide us with news, we are still, surprisingly, not well informed.

But do we really wish to be informed? If this world is so grim, should we not try to shut our ears and eyes, to stay in our bubble and avoid becoming depressed by it all? Can we withstand such a relentless onslaught of bad news? Should we not protect ourselves from it, listen to as little information as possible and do our best to enjoy our ordinary lives?

For many of us, life doesn't seem so bad. No genocide, no earthquake, no tsunami coming down my street. Why bother? *Hakuna matata!* Don't worry, be happy!

How, then, do we educate our children about such news? Do we teach them to close their eyes to the world, too? Whenever they bump into headlines and breaking news, do we tell them that, yes, it is indeed tragic, but there's not much we can do, and it's all happening very far away?

But what if it were the other way round? What if this world appears sinister because we are convinced it is so, and we do not allow ourselves another perspective?

CHAPTER 5

SELF-INDOCTRINATION

WOULD IT BE easier to consider the world so broken that we cannot waste time listening to bad news and should instead just ignore it?

Let's be honest. It doesn't work this way. We are overwhelmed with bad news. The storytelling of the media works mainly, if not exclusively, through presenting bad news.

Should we try to challenge this statement? Are there any big positive events that we can think of in the last decade to balance out the negative ones previously discussed? As the defenders on one side of the boxing ring we have an earthquake, a tsunami, a disaster at a nuclear plant, the suicide of a charismatic actor. Who could step in on the other side of the ring as "good news challenger", and stand a chance of fighting back?

Now, there has to be some good news somewhere in the

last decades. Where is it? We might think it would be more comfortable to ignore the bad news of the world, but it is the good news that we are totally blind to!

How come?

We are trapped in a paradigm. We are trapped in our own perception of the world.

Here is a story inspired by the publications of Paul Watzlawick, an expert researcher in change management[22].

I had tried all available treatments to cure my insomnia, and I was convinced that my case was hopeless. Yet, I decided to make a final attempt and reluctantly consulted a reputable psychotherapist that a friend of mine had recommended.

I was allowed almost the whole of the initial session to explain all my previous unsuccessful attempts to find sleep. At the end of the session I was told: "Your case is indeed desperate, and you will get treatment only if you fully commit to follow the instructions, whatever they may be. Even if, and especially if, some of these orders might sound silly, you must follow them. This is a very sophisticated protocol, so if at any moment you do not respect it, then the course of therapy will be over. This is non-negotiable." I was rather surprised to hear this, but I was impressed by the subtle authority of the psychotherapist, so I agreed. Why not give it a try?

I was given a little envelope. The first order of the protocol was written inside. I was asked to open this envelope only before going to bed and to return to the psychotherapist's office the next morning to receive my second envelop.

When I returned the next day, I was feeling even more desperate than ever. "I'm really sorry," I told the psychotherapist, "I tried as hard as I could but I failed. I haven't been able to follow even the very first order." And I handed back the envelope with the instructions inside.

The psychotherapist replied: "Can you please reopen the envelope, and read the instructions out loud?"

It took me a few minutes to understand that I had, in fact, been cured. I laughed. The psychotherapist smiled back, and concluded: "As you were told, this therapy is now over."

On the piece of paper in the envelope was simply written: "Stay awake."

*   *   *

How did it work? The patient in this story was *actually not* an insomniac. He was trapped by the perception that he was. He was self-indoctrinated. He was *projecting* his vision of the reality upon reality. He had locked himself in a vicious circle from which he could not escape, because his twisted perception had become *self-fulfilling*. The psychotherapist, with his magic envelope, reconnected him with reality. He brought about a paradigm shift by neutralizing the sick pattern of perception in which the patient was locked. The patient was then able to *perceive* reality, instead of *mentally projecting* it. At last, the patient realized that he didn't actually have an issue with sleep.

Unconsciously, this man had nurtured a collection of poisoned messages that were telling him: "You are an insomniac. You are never going to be able to sleep." The little magic envelope disrupted this negative loop.

In a similar fashion, aren't we daily fed with poisoned information that distorts our perception of the world? What if we were *projecting* ugliness onto our world, instead of *perceiving* it as it really is, simply beautiful?

How can we change our own sick paradigm? How can we take a step back? Some of us are trying, but the outcome is not so positive. Wouldn't most of us accept this poison that the world is ugly and cruel, and consider that, in comparison, our day-to-day life is not so bad? What other option do we have but not bother too much about the world, and try to enjoy our lives?

This consists in building a bubble of happiness in a world of sadness. The worse the rest of the world looks, the more our little island shines. What is this called? Individualism. Selfishness. Cynicism. Is it really so appealing?

In political arenas, several leaders have recently used this trick very effectively to attract votes, whether for a referendum or for a presidency. Leave the European Union; build walls; "Make America Great Again"; all these rallying cries follow the same idea of building an island of happiness in an ocean of sorrow.

These same delusions will lead to same disillusions.

*   *   *

Shall we try to reverse the pessimism paradigm?

"Be optimistic about the world." How would that sound?

The issue is that like spontaneity, optimism cannot be commanded. As Watzlawick also brilliantly describes, "be spontaneous!" does not work as an injunction. If ordered to be so, we are no longer spontaneous.

This is why adopting an innocent "positive attitude" is not enough. Optimism cannot be forced; we must let it grow from the inside. We must carefully reject insidiously poisoned information. We must learn to accurately observe reality.

This is where figures help us; they enable us to be more objective in our perception, and better understand our world. They help us to literally "figure it out!"

We only have one world. Shouldn't we give it a chance?

Perhaps we, too, need a paradigm shift that will cure us from our twisted vision of the world, and reopen our eyes to its beauty.

But where could we find our "magic envelope"?

- You are currently holding it in your hands.

Part II

Measuring mankind

Our world is not easy to assess. Why do we tend to focus only on the negative, the catastrophes and the problems?

What if our world is beautiful? What if mankind is actually experiencing much progress?

CHAPTER 6

HOW TO MEASURE MANKIND?

L ET'S ACKNOWLEDGE THAT "measuring" our world is not simple. As an example, it is frequently quoted that half of the Earth's population lives on less than two dollars a day. With that in mind, what would be our best guess for, let's say, the average life expectancy? With such a low level of income, one can assume that half of the global population is unlikely to make it past 35-40 years old? Even balanced against a 70-75 year life expectancy in developed countries, this would lead us to imagine an average global life expectancy of 50-55 years, right? Now let us check the answer. The actual global average life expectancy was 50 years, back in 1960. Nowadays, though, it extends to 71 years[23]. This is surprisingly good news, isn't it?

What a stretch between these two figures: the average income of half of the planet is obviously depressing, whereas the global average life expectancy is a pleasant surprise. So, what should we take into consideration in order to properly measure mankind? Why is our world so difficult to understand? All in all, what is going on?

A first explanation is that it is easier to distribute vaccines than to build schools. Some major improvements have been made on public health issues in developing countries due to international efforts through both public and private organizations. But it takes a generation to make significant progress on education. Similarly, the economy catches up later.

Another explanation is that the first figure about people living on two dollars a day is wrong. Yet, it is still quoted by large international organizations. As an example, in October 2017 it can be found on the website of the serious and credible organization ATD (All Together for Dignity) Fourth World[24]. On a presentation page, they point out that "2.8 billion people, that is to say almost half of the global population, live with less than two dollars per day." It is mentioned that these numbers are derived from United Nations statistics.

Well, both of these figures - the 2.8 billion people living on two dollars a day, and the 6 billion total global population - refer to data from 1996[25]. They are outdated by twenty years. Has the website of ATD Fourth World not been redesigned since, or is this just another convenient way to add a little pessimism that sells better? At least donations for such organizations are for a good cause, but this is, in fact, another misleading measurement of our world.

However, in a more recent UN publication, we are given something interesting: a trend! Please note that whenever is communicated a trend, or a scale, or any comparison of two blocks of data, then it becomes much more meaningful information. Alone, a figure means nothing.

So, according to the 2015 UN Millennium Development Goals report: "Extreme poverty has declined significantly over the last two decades. In 1990, nearly half of the population in the developing world lived on less than $1.25 a day (1.9 billion). That proportion dropped to fourteen percent (836 million) in 2015."

Even though the economy is catching up at its own pace, we are talking of a billion people having escaped from extreme poverty in the last twenty-five years. Is that a trend we have ever noticed? Shouldn't we rejoice over it?

A third explanation for how shortsighted we are when observing our world is that most indicators used to monitor it are economic ones.

How is it that we have had, in the last twenty-five years, such an obvious boom with the Internet and a fifty-six percent reduction in extreme poverty, while facing slack world growth averaging two to four percent per year? The embarrassing and yet plausible explanation is that our main world economic indicators, such as GDP (Gross Domestic Product) growth, are not that relevant.

Why?

* * *

Whether regulated by US GAAP (Generally Accepted Accounting Principles), European IFRS (International Financial Reporting Standards) or other local standards, business accounting remains broadly based on a pattern that dates from the industrial revolution. The model works like this: you buy an industrial machine with your initial capital, you buy raw materials, you spend working hours building a finished product, and you sell it to produce revenue. In your costs you account for the depreciation of the machine, so that you can replace it when it is worn out. The net earnings after tax enable you to pay the stockholders who provided the capital with which you originally bought your machine. If your business is stable, that is it. If it develops, you will increase your capital from the stakeholders and buy another machine. You have a business plan, a breakeven point, and a return on investment. The business itself generates a mechanism of "return on equity" for the stockholders. Everyone is happy.

Now, what if there is no machine? How does one calculate the return on investment, for example, on emails?

As a basic example, let's consider a village composed of ten service providers: one polishes shoes, the second irons shirts, and so on. Each service provider invoices one dollar per service. Let's imagine that, to start with in terms of capital, we only have a single dollar bill in the whole village. We agree that if one full round of services occurs each day, then each service provider earns a dollar daily. Now, what happens if one of the service providers tells his neighbors: "I'm expecting to receive fifty dollars today, so I'd like to have fifty pairs of shoes cleaned." If all the others buy the tale, then each day we have fifty rounds of service instead of one, and each villager earns fifty dollars daily. We now have a community that is fifty times richer, even though we are still speaking of the same unique one dollar bill flying from person to person around the village.

What does this mean? It means that, in a service-oriented economy, wealth is not based on capital but on the number of exchanges that occur. It is a matter of speed. It is a self-sustaining cycle. This can go into a tailspin too: if one player suddenly has doubts, and stops the game for whatever reason, then the bubble bursts. This phenomenon explains our previous market crashes. Recent bubbles were attributed either to debts, or stock markets, or real estate markets - all are linked together anyway. It is not wrong, but it is still too short of an explanation.

The key factor here is the self-sustaining effect. It is neither taken into account, nor even measured. Intuitively, some would call it "trust in the market".

The gap between the industrial age paradigm and the new economy paradigm is the same as that between driving a car and flying a plane. Unlike a car, if a plane accumulates speed, it can fly. But if afterwards it reduces speed too much, it will stall and suddenly drop in altitude. Stock markets have experienced this repeatedly in the last decades.

Now, how stupid would it look if a pilot were asked to fly a plane outfitted with a car's dashboard?

In the same fashion our global economy has entered into a new paradigm which our economic indicators are not fit to describe, because they belong to the past.

Many new businesses have no "machines", so standard accounting does not properly translate their reality, their constraints, or their value. All current accounting, worldwide, is based on "capital". This reflects neither the volume nor the velocity of the "exchanges" which are currently booming and which sustain major, invisible, economic growth.

Phrased differently: when there is no longer a capital associated with most businesses, shouldn't the accounting evolve accordingly? And if the building blocks of financial reporting are inappropriate, then shouldn't we question the economic indicators, such as GDP, that we layer on top?

In the last two decades, we have entered into new economic paradigms. Basic accounting, however, has barely changed at all over the last two centuries. These methods belonged in the industrial age; they are outdated now. This is why economic figures are so misleading[26].

*　　*　　*

If classic economic ratios don't accurately reflect our current reality, then how can we measure our world? Can we think of a situation that is not measured by economic indicators?

When visiting a doctor, you're not asked for your tax report or bank statement, are you? So why is mankind measured only in economic terms? And wrongly measured moreover? At an individual level, health is priceless. Do we have the feeling that the global "health" of mankind is evaluated in any way?

Now we start to understand how blind we are when it comes to assessing our world, and how easily we are misled by the tellers of bad news.

A question that remains unanswered, but has not been forgotten, is the following: how are we to educate our children? Not only are we prevented from creating any distance from bad news, but more distressingly, we are not able to properly introduce our children to the world in which they are growing up. We do not teach them how to love it.

What vision of the world did you inherit, as a child? What vision would you like to bequeath to your children?

A friend of mine had a seven-year-old boy who was going to join a week-long school camp in the Swiss Alps. Most of the children in his class were excited about the week, and were looking forward to it. However, my friend noticed that his son was nervous about the trip. When he asked why, the boy answered: "It's because of this terrible bus accident that we heard about in the news." Three months earlier, a bus returning from a school ski camp in the region nearby had a tragic accident, where twenty-two children died and many others were injured. The dad tried to find a few reassuring words, but mainly he did not know what to say. The following evening, this is what he told his child:

"Let's be honest: this incident was a tragedy, and it was devastating for those involved. Yet this kind of accident happens very rarely, less than once a decade in the whole of Europe[27]. And just here, in Switzerland, do you know how many babies were born on that tragic day[28]? Two-hundred-twenty! For each child that died, ten babies were born, the very same day. So this is life: sometimes tragedies occur, and we should indeed empathize with those affected by such accidents. But we should still live with a sense of joy, because invisibly, there is more to rejoice over than to be sad about."

Surprisingly, the kid got the point.

Now, would we have the faintest idea of how many babies are born in the world each day?

390,000.

Within twelve hours, we have as many babies born globally as people killed in the Haitian earthquake. Even the Rwandan genocide equates to just 2.5 days of global births.

The cumulated death toll of all tragedies previously discussed in this book represents a mere five days of global births.

That's how strongly life prevails over death.

Good news totally outweighs bad news. Are you willing to believe it?

Wait, wait, wait, let's go for the real confrontation here. Let's bring in the past World Wars! As the ever-undefeated defender of bad news, let's recall that champion of bloodbaths, the twentieth century! Come on, baby, knock down this flickering, fragile flame of optimism!

Place your bets...

CHAPTER 7

NEWS FIGHT

S O LET US recall history. Mr. Bad News is packing a fierce punch here. The bell rings, and here is his first throw, a heavy one: the Jewish genocide. Only foolish people would dare deny that this tragedy happened. But are we able to figure out the math on how bad it was? And how does it compare to our previous major blow, the Rwandan genocide, which caused a million fatalities?

The Holocaust resulted is six million fatalities[*]. The Rwandan genocide was four times more destructive than the 2004 Asian Tsunami. But the extermination of the Jewish people was much worse. Six times more devastating than the Rwandan mass killings[29].

---

[*] Broader definitions of the Holocaust that include all minorities persecuted in the Nazi camps total up to 13 million fatalities

Both tragedies have a shocking fatality rate of seventy percent, but the Jewish genocide touches a much larger population of an estimated nine million European Jews at that time. What does that mean, nine million people? To put such figures in perspective, this is roughly the population of New York City, of Quebec province, of Switzerland, or of modern-day Israel. Imagine if seventy percent of the population of any of these places was suddenly wiped out: this is the magnitude of the Jewish genocide.

Another important indicator to consider is the recovery time from such a disaster. How long did it take for the Jewish community to return to the size it was before World War II? We are talking of a seventy year recovery period. Yes, it was only in 2015 that the estimated world Jewish population returned to its pre-Holocaust level of 16 million people[30]. This makes us realize that genocide is a tragedy far beyond what we can imagine. And in the twentieth century, at least two other genocides took place: the one in Armenia in 1915-22, with a death toll of 1.5 million and a seventy-five percent fatality rate[31], and one in Cambodia in 1975-79, with a death toll of two million and a twenty percent fatality rate[32].

Why rifle through the pages of history? Should we not just try to bury this sorrowful twentieth-century, and forget about it?

But how can we understand one of today's most heart-breaking conflicts, between the Jewish and the

Palestinian people, if we are not aware that the effects of the Holocaust have lasted up to today? History helps us figure out the present, and thus build a better future.

Still, Mr. Bad News undoubtedly wins the first round.

*   *   *

So the defender continues into round two, and scores a major blow with the first World War!

Now we are talking of 3.7 times the previous tragedy: World War I resulted in 22 million fatalities, split between 9 million soldiers and 13 million civilians[33]. The world's total population was 1.8 billion at that time[34]. This amounts to 1.2 percent of the world's population dying. This is shocking: WWI was the equivalent of the Haitian earthquake striking two-third of the planet, with the only difference that WWI lasted four years whereas the earthquake that hit Haiti lasted only a few minutes.

In recent conflicts, what might compare to what the WWI soldiers endured? We are talking of 3.3% yearly fatality rate for our WWI soldiers vs 0.5% for soldiers in Iraq[35]. We cannot deny that Iraq was a dangerous playground. World War I was seven times more deadly. Trench warfare was a slaughter.

Second round for Mr. Bad News.

And World War II is not going to look any better. It could be called "World War 3.2" based on its effects. Yes, World

War II was 3.2 times bloodier than World War I, with a total estimated number of 70 million fatalities, split between 20 million soldiers and 50 million civilians[36].

Let's take note that civilian fatalities are much more numerous than military ones. This has been a major pivot in history: in modern conflicts, much more civilians are killed than soldiers.

All in all, this is as though *the entire world population* (2.3 billion people at that time) had faced *one-and-a-half* Haitian earthquakes.

World War II was the equivalent of a 9/11 attack somewhere in the world, for each hour of daylight, seven days a week, over six years. We are talking of 32,000 deaths per day, continuously, over the course of the whole conflict. Put another way, this was like a tsunami striking anywhere in the world, *each week*, continuously during six years.

A total of 1,167 atomic bombs cast on mankind over half a decade.

Mr. Bad News wins round three, and the challenger Mr. Good News is now on the ropes, fading fast.

Where is this leading us? Should we simply bear in mind that the past century was terrible compared to the present and "never complain" because our elders faced more difficult times?

Should we rejoice because today's world is comparably less dreadful than yesterday's?

But then, we are still trapped in our pessimistic vision of the world, aren't we? The past was perhaps worse, but then "worse" could return, right? How can we be confident in any future, if the world was so appalling just half a century ago?

Mr. Bad News is definitely about to win the fight.

*   *   *

"That's all you got?"

Do you remember when Muhammad Ali whispered this to George Foreman, just as the latter was about to win their legendary boxing match on October 30th, 1974? Likewise, beware of Mr. Good News. The fight is not over yet.

We already mentioned the idea of a "recovery time". What would the recovery time be, for these World Wars? Seventy years, like the genocides we considered? Or maybe just twenty years, the equivalent of a generation gap?

Between 1920 and 1940, the world population grew from 1,860 million to 2,300 million[37]. That amounts to a population increase of 22 million per year. So we are talking of a single year of recovery time for World War I.

In the 1950s, world population growth jumped to 50

million a year. That translates to a recovery period of seventeen months for WW II.

Unbelievable, but true: the actual recovery time for each of these devastating World Wars was less than 1.5 years.

This is how robust mankind is.

How old is humanity? If we calculate from the first human writings, officially considered as the start of human history, then humanity is about 5,500 years old. With such a perspective, knowing that the twentieth century World Wars have been the most devastating events we have ever faced, then let's just realize that mankind recovered from them in the blink of an eye.

Both of the twentieth century World Wars combined are a scratch on the skin of our 5,500-year-old humanity.

Mr Good News resoundingly wins the fight. It's a full KO for the Bad News defender. Get this guy out of here, now!

This is called resilience: the ability to pick oneself up again after a blow. And humanity is incredibly resilient. Why are we not more aware of this, and more confident, all in all, about our future?

Why can't we properly figure out the world we live in?

And if this world is finally doing quite well, why do we feel, sometimes, somehow uncomfortable about it?

CHAPTER 8

HARMONY AND MYSTERY

F IGURES ALLOW FOR a better understanding of reality. They enable us to navigate life and look further ahead. They offer perspective beyond immediate information and allow us to consider the bigger picture in an objective manner.

Let's admit that it takes a little work to review past tragedies, to pull out a few figures, and to try to better understand these events. The key here is not just to read the numbers, but to imagine what they mean. Instead of passively absorbing them, we must "get it". We must look at events in 3D and from there feel the motion of our own world.

Why all this effort? What is at stake?

Trust in our future.

Do we actually believe that we are heading in the right direction, that tomorrow will be better than today? Do we really believe in our future? Why is it so difficult to allow such positive outlooks into our mind?

Pythagoras is likely the most famous mathematician of all time. Even though he lived 2,600 years ago, most of us know his name and his famous theorem: "In a right-angled triangle, the square of the hypotenuse is equal to the sum of the square of the two other sides."

What is less known, however, is that Pythagoras believed that numbers were more than just numbers. He had noticed that fractions, when applied to music, were harmonious. Take vibrating cords with the same tension. If their lengths comply with a rational figure, then they generate a harmonious vibration. A three-quarter ratio leads to a musical fourth, a two-third ratio is a fifth, and a half-ratio is an octave. That is to say, if you press on a guitar string exactly in its middle, you get the same note, one octave higher, than the note produced when the string is not pressed.

Pythagoras, along with his whole community, believed that rational numbers (p/q), on which he had built all his mathematical theory, reflected the harmony of the world. He actually believed *in* numbers.

Then, annoyingly, someone asked about a right-angled

triangle in which both sides are identical, let us say equal to one. What is the length of the hypotenuse then?

The guy who dared to ask this question was denounced as a heretic. At that time, it was no laughing matter to be called a heretic, so he was presumably murdered. His name was Hyppasus.

Hyppasus had accidentally discovered $\sqrt{2}$. This did not fit into Pythagoras' mathematical world, which was based on "rational numbers". That is to say, fractions and whole numbers. A rational number is indeed any number that can fit into a "p / q" display (3 being 3/1).

*   *   *

Now, we all know the value of $\sqrt{2}$, by typing on any calculator: 1.4142136. As the number of digits displayed on the screen is limited, we do not realize that there is no repetitive pattern in the decimals after the comma. Just as with the figure π (3.1416), we could fill this entire book with decimals of $\sqrt{2}$, and we would still not nail it down. Any numerical representation of $\sqrt{2}$ is an approximation. As very few people would be interested in knowing that 1.414213562373 is a more accurate version of $\sqrt{2}$ (yet still an approximation, similarly to 3.14159265359 for π), then most of us would not declare it "heretical" that both figures cannot be represented in the form of a "p / q" rational number. They are called "irrational numbers".

Nor do we see why √2 would be such a drama for Pythagoras.

Let's try to put ourselves in his sandals, 2,600 years ago.

Most likely, the demonstration for the Pythagorean Theorem was geometrical. How would this work? In the following example, how can we demonstrate that the area of the big square is equal to the area of the two other squares combined?

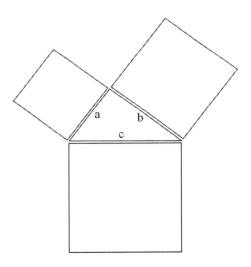

We just have to make everything fit within the big square. For instance, place the right-angled triangle *within* the largest square, from its hypotenuse base, and reproduce this on each side:

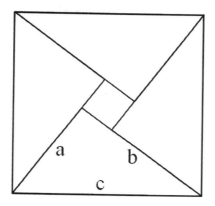

Obviously, the area of the large square is equal to the area of the four triangles plus the square inside. From there, either you take a pair of scissors or you calculate.

Let's calculate, rather than cut up the page of this book to demonstrate! The size of the large square is c^2. Each triangle is $(a \times b / 2)$. The size of the square inside is $(b-a)^2$.

Which translates to $c^2 = 4 \times (ab/2) + (b-a)^2 = 2ab + (b^2 + a^2 - 2ab) = a^2 + b^2$.

A beautiful little mathematical demonstration, isn't it?

Just for the records, with a pair of scissors, four cuts and three moves would be enough:

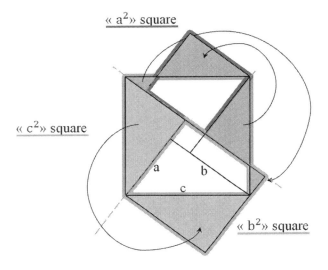

Now what happens with Hyppasus' suggestion? If a = b = 1, then the square in the middle disappears! And so does the previous neat demonstration.

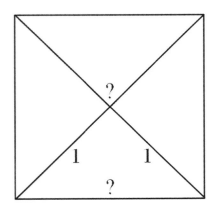

This is why Hyppasus was killed.

In fact, such a question was a major breach in Pythagoras' entire intellectual construction. We are talking of a new mathematical dimension, similar to an object what would surge in 3D from a 2D TV screen. It opens the door to a new paradigm that is actually required to solve the problem.

Now, what is really fascinating in this old story is that the case was rejected. Pythagoras, in fact, had already died by the time Hyppasus asked his question. Still, the Pythagorean community, educated by one of the most brilliant minds in history, did not take interest in the a=b=1 issue. Like the insomniac, they were projecting their own scheme *onto* reality, instead of trying to learn *from* reality. They were scared by what they could not apprehend. They had to live in a world of certainties.

Are we any different, twenty-six centuries later? We do not like what we do not understand. We need certainties. When we reach the edge of our ignorance, we prefer to step back. Why not happily jump ahead?

*   *   *

What if $\sqrt{2}$, for the Pythagoreans, was similar to our world today, for many of us. It frightens us, because we do not comprehend it. We do not try to figure out what is going on, and we retreat in fear instead.

All figures presented in this book so far are easy to find on the internet. Pondering them helps us to better understand our world. Shouldn't we dig under the surface of what the media presents to us as "infotainment", that is to say, poor quality news? Why can't we break free from our addiction to bad news, even though it drives us into inappropriate pessimism?

Aren't we like an ostrich burying its head in the sand? Should we take the risk of looking up?

What if this world were beautiful, yet somehow uncomfortable? What if we are not looking at it in the right light?

Figures enable us to better measure our world, to better assess it. For instance, think of a distance of 40,000 km (25,000 mi): it amounts to about one fifth of a car's lifetime. Many people drive that distance in two years. And yet 40,000km is the circumference of Earth.

Our world is not so big. And we only have one.

Figures enable us not only to understand a reality, but to see *beyond* it. Figures help us to more accurately drive our lives. They allow us to make good decisions, and better educate our kids.

There is no such thing as an ideology or heresy inherent in any figure. There is just an invitation to be more knowledgeable, more aware, and thus improve.

I believe Pythagoras would have loved the $\sqrt{2}$ question, had he still been alive. It would have enabled him to further understand the world he was investigating, and to make progress in his search for harmony.

CHAPTER 9

SENSITIVE FIGURES

S OME FIGURES ARE, however, more difficult to
separate from ideology. Let's consider the next set
of numbers from a purely scientific point of view.
The following lines are meant to be politically neutral,
which is no easy feat considering the topic about to
be discussed.

I bumped into these numbers accidentally, on a World
Health Organization (WHO) web page that mentioned a
twenty-five percent ratio and a 56 million figure[38]. They
are simply too surprising not to be mentioned. They are
also a good example of how figures help to better understand and manage a situation, leaving aside potentially
misleading emotions and ideologies.

What do these two figures refer to? Twenty-five percent is the percentage of induced abortions out of all

pregnancies. 56 million is the total number of abortions, worldwide, per year.

The idea is not to focus too long on this topic. But if we wish to properly "measure" our world, we have to deal with the reality we face. Now that we have entered in this sensitive field, let's study it a little further.

It is an uneasy task to pull out figures or indicators about abortions. Even though the United Nations has a whole agency dedicated to promoting family planning (the United Nations Population Fund), there are very few official statistics available on abortion*. Shouldn't it be an important indicator for family planning, in fact?

In the few statistics that exist about abortion, the ratio commonly used is the "number of abortions per 1,000 women aged 15-44". This ratio is published in a report on "world abortion policies" by the UN Population Division (2013)[39]. Data is available for roughly half of the world's countries, and the values range from five to twenty-five per 1,000, that is to say 0,5% to 2,5%. These numbers seem very low. Is there an error then in the surprisingly high twenty-five percent ratio of induced abortions to all pregnancies? This is bewildering.

What does it mean, *"per 1000 women aged 15-44"*? Here's the trick: in the same spreadsheet, a few columns further along, we find the fertility rate. This one is clear: "average

---

* Except from the Guttmacher institute, a privately founded US organization

births per women over a lifetime". So how is it that in an official UN report, published by experts dedicated full-time to providing this information, we have such an inconsistent presentation of two realities that are so close to one another? The fertility rate is a standard ratio that is easy to understand, with figures available for all countries. Wouldn't it be useful, in order to properly assess the situation, to present the abortion rate the same way? So what is the average number of abortions per woman over a lifetime?

This figure does not seem to be published anywhere. It simply does not exist in any official documents.

*   *   *

Figures about abortion, in the twenty-first century, are like the $\sqrt{2}$ in Pythagorean times. They are completely taboo. Men were sent to the moon five decades ago; shortsightedness can be cured by surgery; bombs are laser-guided; and billions of dollars flow through high-frequency world trade system in seconds. Yet, we have virtually no idea of how abortion impacts the world's women - that is, half the population, in case some decision makers need to be reminded of that fact. Not to mention, by the way, that men are affected by this statistic in same proportions, even though they may be less involved in the consequences.

The twenty-five percent ratio we previously quoted is also misleading. What does twenty-five percent "out of all pregnancies" mean? Have we any idea of the ratio of miscarriages to "all pregnancies", which is also obviously included and which needs to be identified for proper understanding? Where should we go from there?

It is, actually, fairly easy to calculate the average number of abortions per woman over a lifetime. Let us call it the abortion rate, as it is calculated in the same way as the fertility rate. We have a number of births per year and we have a fertility rate. These are available by country, by region, and globally. We have the number of abortions performed annually. This information is official for some countries, and estimated for others, so the consolidated figure remains an estimate. A rule of three, taught at any elementary school, gives the abortion rate.

In a country such as France, where the yearly number of abortions is official, the resulting abortion rate is 0.57. In the US, depending on the source for the number of abortions per year (CDC or Guttmacher Institute), we end up with a rate of 0.31 or 0.44 respectively. In North America, it is 0.51. In Europe, it is 0.86. And globally, it amounts to 1.00[40].

What is the total number of abortions, annually in the world, according to official international organizations? This figure was not found in any UN statistics. 56 million is the latest estimation from both the WHO and the Guttmacher institute.

Eventually, we arrive at an average of 0.5 - 0.8 abortions per woman over a lifetime, in Western countries. Worldwide, the figure of 56 million translates to an average of one abortion per woman over a lifetime.

Wouldn't this mean that the impact of abortion is somehow underestimated? Why so much ignorance?

And why is there so little action to improve the situation?

*   *   *

There is a smokescreen around abortions, and related figures are often misleading. When provided, they are not "scaled". For instance, the rate of maternal deaths resulting from unsafe abortion (47,000 out of 21.6 million)[41] is rarely compared to the total average maternity death rate, from all causes (303,000 out of 142 million)[42]. Both rates are actually similar: 0.218% versus 0.213%. This argues for a more comprehensive approach. Also, there seems to be no real scientific studies on the potential psychological consequences of abortion. "Scientific" here means neutral, reproducible, based on figures and validated by the scientific community. More precisely, most of the numerous studies about abortion from official psychiatric organizations, which conclude there are no such consequences, seem to be qualitative only - there are not quantified with figures. The only study based on figures (from Pf Coleman in 2011) reached a very different conclusion, which was much criticized afterwards, and it has not been reproduced[43].

How, then, to comment on such a topic? Allow me a few thoughts.

First, let us acknowledge how difficult it is to approach this topic without having an emotional bias or ideological interference (pro-choice vs. pro-life). This can obviously jeopardize objective and dispassionate thinking.

Second, abortion rate estimates* are lower in developed countries than in developing ones. This is surprising. As an approximate statement (cultural bias and other factors would need to be taken into account): the less medically assisted the area, the higher the rate. This seems to indicate that a legal and safe abortion strategy does not generate a higher number of abortions performed. This is important to note, when complications with unsafe abortions are estimated at twenty to fifty percent, and are potentially severe.

And lastly, scientifically speaking, one cannot deny that the "entity" potentially subject to being aborted is alive (it is not an object). And if nothing is done, it will become a human being. This is even the issue, to be honest. Setting aside the global statistics, which might be imprecise, if we simply focus on the figures related to Western countries this means that currently the first nine months of a human being's life is subject to a twenty to thirty percent

---

* Figures are estimates in most non-western countries

fatality rate (0.5-0.8 abortion for approximately two births). To understand what such numbers mean, let's recall the yearly fatality rate for the Coalition soldiers in Iraq: that was 0.5%.

In our twenty-first century Western world, an embryo is forty times more at risk of being aborted than a soldier in a warzone is of being killed. In a few centuries, won't people look back at us and consider our times as the equivalent of the Middle Ages, on this issue? Without blaming anyone at the individual level, at a societal level should such a reality be considered as acceptable?

In a nutshell, from a mathematical point of view, both pro-life and pro-choice perspectives are, simultaneously, right and wrong. Legal safe abortion needs to be available. It is a health concern, and it does not seem to have "ideological consequences" - it likely does not generate more abortions. Adequate aftercare in the form of optional psychological follow-up should also be included. Yet such high numbers are embarrassing, and we should aim at progressively reducing them.

Would a two percent yearly decrease really be so difficult to achieve? We do not even try.

Would we wish our best friend to have an abortion?

Given these statistics, the issue seems to hit *every other one of our daughters*. Do we really wish to pass this on, as such, to the next generation?

If this were a business process, this would typically be addressed not in production, but in research and development. The resolution of a recurrent problem always lies upstream.

The issue is not about the decision of whether or not to abort. It is how to avoid unwanted pregnancies.

There are currently massive efforts to make family planning accessible worldwide, so what is the problem? Well, here is the situation: whereas the abortion rate in developed countries seems to have stabilized at a high level, not only are there no targets to decrease it, but it's not even a "key indicator", nor is it properly measured!

Why? Let's venture an explanation. Since abortion is a politically sensitive issue, it is hidden among other "family planning" policies. Consequently, family planning is somehow considered a three-topic program: education, contraception, abortion.

Abortion should be considered as a different subject. It is not just "part three" of the program. It is a failure of education and contraception. It is, in fact, *the* failure of the program.

Why is it not being measured, and managed, as such?

Now, let's try to close this chapter peacefully. This topic also tells us something about mankind. We are imperfect.

That's our beauty, somehow. That's how we progress.

CHAPTER 10

AN UNBELIEVABLE TRUTH

WHERE DO WE stand? Humanity is resilient when it comes to tragedies, even those such as the World Wars of the past century. Great! Measuring reality sometimes leads to some uncomfortable figures, worth further analysis. OK. All in all, should we have faith in our world? Or should we bury our heads back in the sand, presuming that there is really nothing we could have an impact on?

Fatalism is a close neighbor to pessimism. How does one escape from that murky area?

In the previous chapters of this book, we developed a scale that helps us to understand most events. But we do not have the global picture yet, do we? We still know very little about how mankind is doing. Where is the "blood pressure"?

Where is the "heart beat"? Where are the key figures that would enable us to have an idea of mankind's "health"?

Let's keep counting.

What do we know at this stage? The daily number of births is 390,000, worldwide. This is the equivalent of two Haitian earthquakes, each day, birth-wise. The increase in the world population is 82 million a year. This seems big, doesn't it? Indeed, it is almost the equivalent of the number of fatalities from both World Wars combined. And it's more than the population of any European country (Germany has 80 million people; France, UK and Italy stand around 60 to 65 million each).

Yet, I still do not "get it". This is not so meaningful, is it? What is missing?

We are comparing apples with oranges. These are numbers of people, sure, but they do not relate to a similar reality. We cannot "compare" yet. So let us run some additional calculations.

What is the current world population? 7.5 billion, and counting. So how does this yearly 82 million increase translate as a percentage? It amounts to 1.1%. This does not seem so high after all.

Let's double-check. What is the total number of deaths in the world, each year? 60 million. How does that translate per day? 164,000.

What should I conclude, if I compare all these figures? They do not match!

How could we have 60 million deaths and a population increase of 82 million, each year, worldwide? How can we count 390,000 births and 164,000 deaths, each day, globally? There must be a mistake somewhere in these numbers!

There is none. These figures are accurate[44].

Now this is getting really confusing. How do we go about sorting this out?

* * *

Currently, the total number of births in the world is 2.4 times higher than total number of deaths.

Daily, 390,000 births versus 164,000 deaths. Yearly, 142 million versus 60 million. This is unbelievable, yet true.

What does it mean? We are presently experiencing an incredible moment of growth in mankind, as never experienced before in our whole 5,500-year history.

As a first comment, like in any romantic movie, we can happily say that life is stronger than death. Yet, two and a half times stronger... This might be a little too much, perhaps?

It is. As any Chief Executive Officer (CEO) from a booming business would testify, a little growth is always welcome, but strong growth usually translates to a major challenge for a company. So is it for humanity.

Here, we finally understand why we are simultaneously doing very well, and yet feeling "somehow uncomfortable".

Mankind is currently facing a *crisis of growth*.

Are we aware of this?

*   *   *

What shall we do from here? Believe in our world, in a kind of forced optimism. Or be scared and hide?

Think? Or prepare ourselves to sink? Cheer or brace for impact?

Put differently: is this good news or bad news?

"If crisis of growth there is, able to manage it are we?" The Jedi master Yoda might phrase it thus. "Huuumm…" Would he enigmatically proceed. Usually, at this moment of the movie, it means we are in big trouble.

Are we? Honestly, can we afford such growth? Where is this leading us to?

In future, will we all fit on Earth? Are we growing, quantity-wise, but simultaneously deteriorating, quality-wise? Are we not just about to burst the planet?

Last but not least, how do we explain this situation to

our kids? How do we educate them, apart from teaching them Chinese, because we are afraid that this is where all business will inevitably be delocalized?

Is mankind heading full speed towards a wall?

The only answer available now, is: we do not know.

We are like these Pythagorean disciples, facing a $\sqrt{2}$ case. We are on the edge of our own ignorance. We have a breach in all our previous paradigms. And this is exactly why we are uncomfortable about our world. How many of us are just frightened about our future? Are you?

Yet, there is an answer to bring to the table. A trail that we could blaze together.

Shall we?

Part III

A crisis of growth, or a unique momentum?

CHAPTER 11

HOW ARE WE DOING, GLOBALLY?

LET'S EXPLORE THIS question. Imagine if someone were to knock at our world's door, and casually ask humanity: "How are we doing, today?" What would be the answer?

Are we misinformed? Mismanaged? Miserable? There is something amiss in this world, isn't there? But what is it?

The world economy is growing. Slowly. The main indicator we have for this is the Gross Domestic Product (GDP). Allow me to elaborate a little more on this. Would anyone but an expert be able to explain how the GDP is calculated? For instance, how do public administrations contribute to it? If I replaced the village of shoe-polishers, in my previous example, with one inhabited by public administration clerks who, instead of providing a service, control each other - a village of IRS auditors, let's say - would it generate the same GDP?

If yes, then a country can artificially boost its GDP just by multiplying the administrative controls of its business activities. I'm not sure that represents any economic growth.

If not, then what about the added value of the auditing companies known as the "Big Four"? This is an example of administrative control. They definitely form part of the GDP as private companies, and are usually listed on the stock market. Does that mean that a control process is GDP-contributing when private, and not when public?

Tax directly translates as revenue for use in public administration. Does such revenue count as part of the GDP? If so, it can be added in artificially. Otherwise, how does one calculate the added value of a public administration? From its spending? Are administration expenses really an added value? This does not make sense: if an administration spends twice as much money due to inefficiency, it does not properly contribute to the growth of a country's economy. And when public spending represents twenty-nine to fifty-seven percent of a country's GDP, such an obvious calculation bias raises serious questions about GDP,[45] doesn't it?

The limits of measuring national incomes were identified

at the outset by Simon Kuznets, the economist who first researched this topic. In his report to the US congress in 1934, he noted that, "With quantitative measurements especially, the definiteness of the result suggests, often misleadingly, a precision and simplicity in the outlines of the object measured. Measurements of national income are subject to this type of illusion and resulting abuse." In other words, GDP is a useful indicator, but it is misleading when used as an absolute reference, because it does not reflect the complexity of a country's economy. In fact, it was never meant to be "accurate".

*   *   *

Here is an actual conversation that occurred between two top mathematicians looking at the Golden Gate Bridge. After a few minutes of reflection, the first said: "The curve of the upper main cable is a cycloid." He was referring to the curve a fixed point on a bicycle wheel makes as the wheel turns. The second answered candidly, "Oh come on! It cannot be periodical, because the bridge can be extended indefinitely." To calculate such a curve, meant to equally spread the load over each vertical cable, requires real mathematical expertise. To understand the second mathematician's refutation, though, is quite straight forward, as this drawing demonstrates:

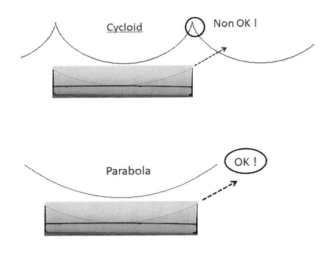

Suspension bridge design

Sometimes all it takes is a little common sense to under-stand that a complex calculation is wrong. Quite often also, the less complicated the model, the more relevant it is. In the previous suspended bridge example, the correct answer is a simple parabola $y = cx^2$.

No one dares to challenge the ubiquitous use of GDP because only experts understand how it is calculated, and like our first mathematician, experts are often too close to the problem they are addressing to see the flaws.

Like with the suspended bridge, can a complex calcula-tion such as GDP be called into question by a simple argument? Let me try to illustrate why this indicator is not only inaccurate, as public spending reveals, but is also irrelevant today.

Take the example of an international phone call. A few decades ago, placing such a phone call was expensive. It could cost as much as two dollars a minute. When you remember that, at the time, half the global population was living on less than two dollars a day, a thirty minute overseas phone conversation was definitely pricey. Yet, some people were placing such phone calls, obviously considering that their conversation was worth the sixty dollars.

Now, if you reduce the cost by ninety percent, the very same phone call is billed at six dollars. Does the added value of the conversation decrease in any way? No. Moreover, with a lower cost, you will even make more phone calls, have more conversations, and create more added value. Let us say that you now place three similar phone calls, for a total cost of eighteen dollars. The contribution to GDP diminishes by seventy percent. But the activity measured grows by a factor of three.

Now imagine if phone calls were free, unlimited, and could carry a thousand times more information in less time. With such an unbelievable improvement, we would need to find another name for such communications. How about calling them, um, "e-mails"! If you exchange 300 emails a day with spreadsheets, presentations, a thesis, or a link to your latest vacation pictures for your friends, then what is the resulting contribution to GDP? Nothing! With a low subscription price per month, the cost per unit of communication becomes insignificant.

The price of the "phone call" decreased by 99%. But the point of this illustration is that the added value never was in the cost of the call. It was in the conversation.

The economy of the twenty-first century is based neither on capital, nor on cost, value-added, or any of the elements tracked in accounting and in GDP.

It is based on information. *Nowhere is it accounted for.*

*   *   *

So much for the key indicator of national and global economic growth. Where does this leave us? Even though the speed indicator of the plane is defective, how good is the pilot?

Our political elite? In a globally connected world, how many are fluent in at least one other language? How many have lived a year or more abroad? Very few, unfortunately, and the rest demonstrate less international experience than most of today's young business school graduates. In any case, some within the political elite capitalize on people's fears by promoting such old-fashioned and ineffective ideas as protectionism, or even nationalism. On the other hand, the "non-populist" political leaders, who are supposedly brilliant and inspired, have a tough time winning elections against the former group. In this global world, all are somehow lost.

Our business leaders? One of them made his multi-billion dollar fortune within a decade by stealing student pictures from his business school, and business plans from two other "friends" who had placed their trust in him. Now, not only is he welcomed among the world's top influencers, but he has access to the private data of one fifth of the world's population. Great!

Others do create and finance private organizations, such as the Bill & Melinda Gates Foundation, which has a budget equivalent to that of the WHO (four billion dollars per year). And Bill regularly tries to explain that "the world is doing much better than what people usually think." Let's not criticize the extraordinary entrepreneurial and philanthropic work of Bill and Melinda Gates, among others. And yet...

And yet, we would need, from whichever elite, a vision, a direction, a plan.

The UN tries to provide something. We currently have seventeen "sustainable development goals" up and running. But, this is so like the UN…It's not a vision! Nor is it the effective communication of a strategy! Would we be able to quote three of these seventeen goals? Or even one?

And while we are so poorly informed and managed at global level, we are facing a crisis of growth, a major moment in the history of mankind. Let's make this an opportunity. Together, can't we do better than this little elite club?

Some people are used to not taking action, waiting instead for whichever charismatic leader will show them the way. This is the "savior" syndrome. Some feel unhappy and blame it on "the others". This is the "enemy" syndrome. Political populism combines both: "I am the savior and I am going to protect you from the European Union / Mexicans / China / whatever is outside."

Both the savior and enemy syndromes are childish attitudes.

As John F Kennedy said, "Let us accept our own responsibility for the future."

*   *   *

All right, if we are in charge, instead of the elite, what should we do? If we were the joint CEOs of the world, how would we build the best strategy from here?

In *the Art of War*, famous military strategist Sun Tzu insists that any strategy must be based on the best prior assessment of the situation. Evaluate, evaluate, evaluate. We must keep inquiring: what is going on; what is this all about? Whether in business, military or therapeutic practice, any strategy begins with a thorough understanding and measuring of the field.

This brings us back to the initial question of this chapter: how are we doing, globally?

We do not know.

Actually, we might even ignore the question itself: is it being asked, anywhere in the news or in political debates?

We are trapped in the murky waters of ignorance, hence we are pessimistic.

Perhaps, we don't even try to know how our world is doing, because we believe upfront that we cannot understand it. We throw in the towel before even trying. Pessimistic and therefore ignorant. Ignorant and therefore pessimistic... How can we break out of this circle of self-indoctrination?

How are we doing, globally? The real question is actually: *do we want to know?*

Maybe not. In which case this book is useless. Toss it out. But what if you were curious about some answers that can really shift your perspective?

In the dark, a spark is enough to light a candle and brighten a whole room.

So let's cast a spark on our world.

CHAPTER 12

THE BIG PICTURE

L ET'S STEP BACK and take another look at the big picture for mankind. Our world population is currently 7.5 billion people, with a yearly net growth of 82 million, resulting from 142 million births and 60 million deaths. Wow.

Has anyone presented such figures to us? Were we given any explanation, or any plan for the future? Have demographics been mentioned in any recent political campaigns?

There is no doubt that we are facing a crisis of population growth. How should we think about this?

Where will such growth lead us? Will we all fit on the planet eventually? Should we prepare to evacuate to Mars?

First of all, let's consider the growth curve itself. It is exponential or asymptotic? That is to say, is it going to increase with no limit, or stabilize at some maximum level?

Demography is a straightforward problem from a mathematical point of view. There are two variables to take into account: fertility rate and life expectancy. That's enough to calculate the future size of our population. Think of this like inventory: if you know your current level, what is coming in and how long it will stay, then you know how the stock will evolve. From there, you can tell whether it will ultimately fit in the warehouse or not.

The good news is that both fertility rate and life expectancy are closely monitored by the UN. Many statistics are available on this topic. Scenarios are calculated, and published, about how the world population can develop in different ways. The bad news is that, though available, this information is not so well communicated to the public. Also, such figures are only estimates. Perhaps the latter explains the former: people expect certainties. Leaders are not so brave at proclaiming "this is our best guess about where we're heading..."

In such scenarios, estimates of the total world population in 2100 vary from 9.7 billion to 13.5 billion. There is a ninety-five percent chance that we will fall within this range, which still means a forty percent gap between the low and high levels. The medium scenario leads to a population of 11.4 billion.

Here are the curves:

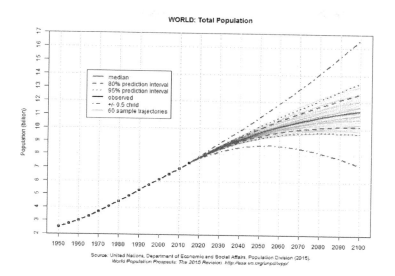

Source: United Nations, Department of Economic and Social Affairs, Population Division (2015). World Population Prospects: The 2015 Revision. http://esa.un.org/unpd/wpp/

Estimates of future world population[46]

If we carefully consider the graph, the questions we are asking prove to be relevant, and possibly frightening. Will our world population eventually stabilize, or keep increasing? Will we all fit into this global warehouse of ours called Earth?

*   *   *

Will such growth stabilize? Look at the previous curve: the median estimate, in the middle, seems to stabilize with an asymptote, that is to say a maximum level, of 11-12 billion people. The remaining fifty percent chance upper scenarios seem to either keep growing, or even become exponential (that is, the increase itself increases). Should we feel half assured and half alarmed? Let's try to understand this further, by working separately on each of the two demographic variables: fertility rate and life expectancy.

Fertility rate is an easy one to tackle. And 2.0 is the key value to keep in mind, equivalent to a stable population replenishment (technically, it is in fact 2.1). Currently the global average is 2.5, but the trend keeps decreasing. Families are having fewer children. Here, we have a solid correlation with another trend, that of economic development. In developed countries, fertility rate is currently below 1.9, versus 2.6 in developing countries (except in Africa, where it is 4.7).

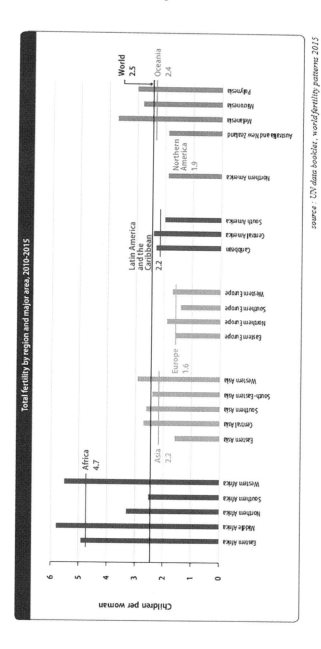

Fertility rate by region[47]

As developing countries continue to join the developed countries club, we can assume that the global fertility rate will finally drop to the 2.0 value that stabilizes the population. How quickly will it decrease? The UN estimates that the rate of 2.2 will be reached by 2050, and the rate of 2.0 by 2090.

We can consider that estimations of the fertility rate are solid, and that, if it were the only variable to take in account, the world population will definitely stabilize pretty soon.

So the uncertainty lies in the second variable: life expectancy. How does that look? How is it likely to evolve? Here is the related curve:

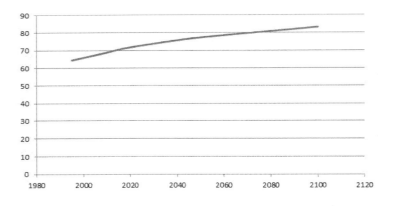

Life expectancy (in age) by year (1990 - 2100)[48]

Here we have an issue. In this curve there is no obvious upper limit that appears. Life expectancy seems to keep increasing. Regularly. Persistently.

The more developed the country, the higher the level of technological development in healthcare, vehicle safety, etcetera, which seemingly points to an endless increase in life expectancy.

Yet, if we reflect on this, we can uncover some clues about this pattern. As a matter of fact, it will become more and more difficult to increase life expectancy beyond its natural limits. The oldest person currently alive is a major indicator of a "natural limit": out of a world of seven billion inhabitants, we have a tiny number of people who reach 115 years old. Continuous improvement in health will enable a population to get closer to this age. But to go beyond means to beat a seven-billion case statistic, and that would require major technological leaps. Even if such technology is developed, it is likely to spread slowly given the likelihood of its high costs.

We can therefore assume that global life expectancy will either stabilize at a maximum level, or keep growing but at a very slow pace. In fact for the whole twenty-first century, life expectancy is expected to increase from 66 to 83 years old. This is a mere twenty-six percent gain. It does not impact our "global inventory" that dramatically.

As the former variable fertility rate is expected to stabilize soon, so should the world population. Furthermore, technology will also enable us to more accurately drive the combination of these two variables with better family planning, education, and so on. In developed countries the anticipated trend is actually that programs will have to be promoted to counter a declining fertility rate. So most likely we are heading toward an asymptote eventually.

From a different perspective, we can reach the same conclusion: the most sensitive variable of the two is the fertility rate. Indeed, life expectancy is the duration in the warehouse: if it doubles, the stock doubles, no more. Whereas the fertility rate leads to an exponential curve if it does not stabilize. If we have three births instead of two, the next generation results in 4.5 births (3x 3/2), instead of two. There is a compound ratio effect.

To conclude, here is the good news: our world population is heading towards a maximum level (i.e. an asymptote). The bad news: we do not know its final size, nor when it will be reached.

Whether we stabilize in 30, 50 or 200 years is not really the question. Whether we will all fit on our planet is. Where does such growth ultimately lead us?

The median scenario, which we occasionally hear about, leads to a final 11-12 billion population. That is a sixty percent increase from our current 7.5 billion world population! This already sounds quite worrying, doesn't it? What about the high estimate?

*   *   *

Currently the highest scenario, within a 2.5% chance of

probability, would bring our world population to 13.5 billion in 2100. What does such a figure evoke? The question is not so much about the number, but about the resulting situation. What does it mean, in fact, to live in a world populated by 13.5 billion people? Would it look like the subway during rush hour?

Surprisingly, this is a fairly easy question to work out by considering the population density. The current 7.5 billion world population translates into 57 inhabitants per square kilometer, globally[49]. Assuming that the viable surface area on Earth remains unchanged (with no potential habitation on or under the surface of oceans taken into account), then the 14 billion "high" scenario leads to a population density of 106 people per square km. Let's be awfully pessimistic, and go for twice the previous "high" estimate: 28 billion people on Earth would equal a density of 212p/km2. How jam-packed would this be?

Well, 106p/km2 is slightly below the current average population density in the European Union (121p/km2). And 212p/km2, our awfully pessimistic scenario, is the population density of Switzerland. The latter is a beautiful country, with Alpine mountains, important agricultural activity, and a pattern of midsize cities that are pleasant to live in. Swiss cities have very few skyscrapers. There are some traffic issues here and there, but nothing compared to New York City, London, or Paris. In fact, Switzerland is regularly quoted as one of the best places in the world to live!

Yes, we will all fit! Even with a final world population of 28 billion, which is twice the level of the UN's high scenario, and very unlikely to occur. We do fit into what can still be a beautiful and balanced environment.

So perhaps this crisis of growth isn't such a big deal, after all? Finally, we are only talking of a population increase of a 1.1% a year? And besides, our Earth "warehouse" is suitably large enough to accommodate four times our current "stock" of inhabitants, right?

Let's check the population curve, to better understand the situation. Usually, the data is available either from the past to the present (historical data), or from the present to 2100-2300 (projected data). How would both look combined? Here it is:

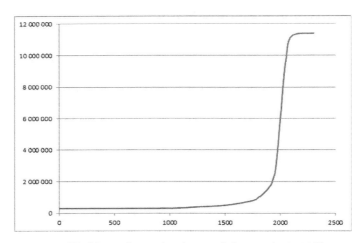

World population (in thousand) by year (1-2300)[50]

Isn't such a growth curve stunning? Let's try to figure this out.

*   *   *

Three times in two centuries mankind has doubled in size. Between 1850 and 1950: the world's population increased from 1.26 billion to 2.5 billion. Then, in the 1980s, it jumped to five billion. And it is expected to reach ten billion by the 2050s.

Such a curve might seem familiar to some parents. Doesn't it look like a teenager's growth spurt? Could humanity be in an adolescence phase?

Let's take a glance at the growth curve of a teenager. Between the ages of ten and sixteen years old, the average teenager grows from about 140cm (55 inches) to 175cm (69 inches). This seems amazing to any parent, yet it is only an increase of twenty-five percent over six years (so thirty-seven percent of the lifetime of a sixteen year old kid).

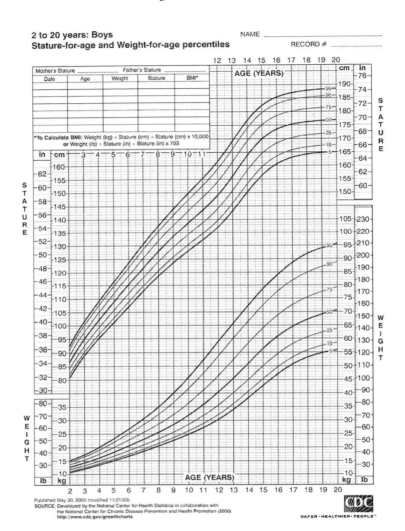

Teenage growth curve[51]

Doubling in size occurs only once in the life of a human being. This takes place between the ages of two and seventeen years old.

Within two centuries, the equivalent of four percent of human history, or eight months for a seventeen-year-old human being, humanity has doubled in size three times. Yes, we are talking of four times* the growth of a child from age two to seventeen, within the equivalent of eight months of its life.

Let's rephrase this, focusing on the teenage growth spurt. Mankind grew 28 times more (700% vs 25%), and 9.4 times faster (2/50 centuries vs 6/16 year), than a child between ten to sixteen years old**.

This is as though a ten-year-old child would become 11m tall (430 inches, or higher than a three-floor building) before the age of eleven! That's quite a vigorous kid, isn't it?

Mankind is experiencing a teenage crisis that is 260 times more intense than an individual human adolescent's.

Ha! Now we see the problem. Now we understand why we sometimes feel "uncomfortable".

---

* Mathematically indeed, three times a two-fold increase is actually an eight-fold increase, as 2x2x2 = 8. This translates to a 700% increase from the initial level.

** If mankind is apprehended as a volume (body) or as a surface (globe), then the resulting 260x ratio is to be pondered by a cube root or square root factor, which leads to 6.4x or 16x. Yet, this is still amazing.

But would you tell your teenager that his or her growth is "a problem"? Yes, it is uncomfortable sometimes, but it is still a unique moment in a human being's life. It is the fascinating transition time when a child becomes an adult. It is a magic moment when the first big decisions are to be taken, and maturity is to be acquired.

And this is where we currently stand.

But is there anyone in the world "situation room" dealing with this challenge? Honestly, we could spend a lifetime staring at these five words and still not grasp what they actually imply:

The Adolescent Crisis of Humanity.

CHAPTER 13

CAN WE HANDLE IT?

HUMANITY IS EXPERIENCING an intense teenage moment, concentrated into the few decades we are currently living through.

Can we handle it? So far, we don't even seem to be aware of it. As strategists, we are not only missing an evaluation of the situation, we haven't even asked for one!

Let's think this through. Such a fast growth pattern explains why progress happens at a jerky pace. If you consider any fast-growing business, it looks shiny from the outside, but on the inside it is usually a bit of a mess. Because even though management does its best to adjust the processes and the internal tools to sustain the growth of the business, whatever is conceived today is already skimpy by the time it becomes operational. If not, then it will be soon after.

Likewise, if vaccines are distributed in a developing country today, then schools should be prepared for the increase in population, tomorrow. Roads should be laid for the day after that. Buildings must be constructed the following week. However, such activities are not managed by the same organizations, and hence are not coordinated. Are they even planned or foreseen? The project for a new highway is initiated once the previous route has already being saturated for a while. And it takes another lengthy period to build the road. So we keep catching up. We follow growth; we rarely manage or anticipate it.

Surely, vaccines are easier to distribute than schools are to build. And yet, schools are still easier to build than teachers are to train.

As the saying goes: "Give a man a fish, and he will eat for a day; teach a man to fish, and he will eat for a lifetime." The key to figuring out our messy kind of growth is to consider the second degree angle: how can we best train the "fishing teachers"? And actually, the real strategic question lies in the third degree angle: how can we scale up the "train the trainers" program? Could a self-training program for potential "fishing trainers" be envisioned?

The third degree is a little foggy, yet important to understand. It is the acceleration of the acceleration. If you open the door to self-training, then it is the whole country that eats for a lifetime.

In other words: it is strategically more important to teach

progress than to simply enable progress. But then, what about *accelerating* the teaching itself?

What if people were able to access a self-progress-enabling platform? What if potential teachers had access to all self-training programs, worldwide, at their fingertips?

Hello, Internet!

* * *

Fish enable us to eat. Books enable us to grow.

In this proverb, replace the fish with a book, and the fishing line becomes a school. In both cases, the challenge is to train the teachers. Then here we have been granted a worldwide trainers academy in the form of Massive Open Online Courses, many of which are currently available and more being developed every day. MOOCs are online courses from schools and universities that enable education in a number of fields at any level.

Nowadays, you can graduate from a top-level MBA online. Soon, all MBAs and most university programs will be available online. The possibility of becoming a teacher, a doctor, a lawyer, or an engineer, is now as close as a keyboard and a screen.

We are in the Information Age. The real and major stake is access to information. Once access is ensured, the acquisition of knowledge will naturally grow from itself. Knowledge is a strange beast: it is simultaneously the fish, the teacher and the academy. Knowledge is like a beautiful octopus that climbs a ladder with half of its eight arms while at the same time building the next rungs with the other four. Some people just need access to a little information to "get it", and then train their whole village. They are the self-made men and women of the future. All they need, to get started, is access to the Internet.

To estimate whether we can handle the amazing growth of humanity boils down to one question: is knowledge growing fast enough? If humanity is a teenager, then does her brain develop as fast as her body?

Is the Internet spreading fast enough?

How can we step back and assess where we are with the Internet? It has been around for a while now, about twenty-five years since the beginning of the "world wide web" (1991). A quarter of a century! And yet, wars and conflicts are still going on. Education is still mainly in schools. Medical therapy is still performed at doctors' office and in hospitals. As a venture capital firm tersely wrote: "we wanted flying cars, instead we got 140 characters." Is the Internet a disappointing dream?

Let's call on history again. How does the Internet compare with the last major technological leap in information, namely the printing revolution?

In a few centuries, will people remember the arrival of the

Internet as an invention as revolutionary as the Gutenberg printing press?

* * *

So here we go for another little competition. The defender is the traditional world of books, whether hand-written (manuscript before Gutenberg) or fresh off the printing press. The challenger is the Internet.

How should we keep score? The Internet and books do not fight against each other, they run alongside one another. We are not in a boxing ring this time. This competition is based on speed. We are on an athletic race track. Which of these sprinters will win?

Our chronograph works like this: it measures how fast *each can multiply itself by ten times.*

Indeed, the idea is to understand how rapidly humanity was impacted by each of these knowledge-enhancing technologies.

For example, in the sixth century, books were accessed by roughly 1 out of 150,000 people[*]. By the eighth century, it was 1 in 50,000. By then, it took two centuries for books to become three times more accessible[52].

How long did it take for books to spread by a factor of ten?

---

[*] By "access to books", we mean the average consumption of one book per year

Before Gutenberg, a tenfold increase in book accessibility took four to six centuries. Progress occurred during the Middle Ages when monks at monasteries specialized in hand-writing manuscripts (mainly the Bible). The fastest "x10 spread" took about 3.5 centuries (one person out of 10,000 had access to books by the mid-eleventh century, then it was one in 1,000 in the fifteenth century).

Right before Gutenberg's printing press invention in the middle of the fifteenth century, an average of one in 300 people had access to books in Europe.

Thanks to Gutenberg's revolutionary machine, within a century, this became one out of 30. Then it took about two more centuries to make it one in three[53].

What about the Internet? Of course access to the Internet provides much more information than a book per year, but well, this is the challenger! It's normal that he is slightly disadvantaged by the rules, right?

By mid-1993, one person in 300 had access to the Internet, worldwide. It took 4.5 years to make this one in 30. Then another thirteen years (1998 to 2011) to make it one in three.

If we compare both of these technologies, the 1/300 to 1/30 spread (increase in access to information) took only 4.5 years for the Internet to achieve, versus a century for Gutenberg's press. After that, the 1/30 to 1/3 spread took a mere thirteen years for the Internet, versus two hundred years for Gutenberg.

The Internet revolution spread twenty times faster than Gutenberg's Printing Revolution.

In a hundred-meter sprint race, the Internet challenger crosses the line ninety-five meters ahead of Gutenberg. The fellow defender cannot run more than five meters before the race is over.

And let's no longer omit the increase of knowledge and resources available *within* the Internet, which also made tremendous progress within these two timeframes (1993-1998, then 1998-2011). Here we have the "square" of an exponential growth: *both* the numbers of people accessing the Internet and the size of the available "bookshelf" are booming.

It is not an easy task to estimate the increase of information available on the Internet, because "information" and "bytes" are not exactly correlated. For instance, a picture takes more and more storage capacity over the years due to a better quality in resolution, but it does not really increase the "information" that the picture conveys. Yet let's have a quick look at Internet traffic. Since 1992, traffic increased roughly by ten to twenty times over each period of five years, with one remarkable exception. From 1997 to 2002 it exploded by 3,600 times! Indeed, in 1997 Internet traffic was estimated at 100 Gigabytes per hour. In 2002, that became 100 Gigabytes per second[54]. Calculated differently, when it comes to the number of Internet hosts, it grew by sixteen times from mid-1993 to 1998, then by twenty-five times over the next thirteen years[55].

Therefore, if we consider the spread of access (twenty times faster) multiplied by the volume of data accessed (way beyond twenty times larger within each of these time spans, 1993 to 1998 and 1998 to 2011), then we can undoubtedly conclude that the Internet has produced a knowledge-sharing revolution that is at the very least 400 times more effective than the Gutenberg revolution.

In our whole human history, the Internet revolution is by far the event that has had the biggest impact. It has been the most extraordinary invention ever, since the development of writing. *And it is our generation that is experiencing this major turning point in the evolution of mankind.*

The good news is that, yes, knowledge is developing faster than humanity grows. In other words, our ability to solve issues is growing faster than the issues that will arise.

So now we are able to honestly answer the original question: can we handle such a crisis of growth? Right now, perhaps not. Tomorrow, undeniably yes, given how fast our global knowledge is developing.

CHAPTER 14

WHO IS IN CHARGE?

S O WE ARE facing a crisis of growth, 260 times more disruptive than a teenager's growth spurt. But luckily we are also experiencing an amazing increase of "global knowledge", which is developing faster than our population grows. It seems we should be able to handle it. Right?

Let's not skip an embarrassing question, though: are we actually able to manage such an increase of knowledge?

Teenagers are like different kinds of birds, and the way each flies is something of a mystery. At the same age, some teenagers can train for the Olympics, while others dabble in drugs. Many, still, are more or less fairly balanced. Some run while others smoke. What makes a kid fall into one category instead of another? The decisions he or she takes.

Our teenage humanity might be offered the equivalent of a good school, in terms of knowledge acquisition. But does maturity follow? What about her decision-making abilities?

Roger Penrose, a brilliant British mathematician, illustrates this nicely in a short story[56]. Some of the planet's cleverest minds had built *the* computer, called "Ultronic", able to answer *any* questions. During the official inauguration of "Ultronic" in front of a massive assembly, the presenter asked, "Would anyone like to submit the first question?" No one dared to respond. How would one imagine, and publicly phrase in front of such an impressive audience, a question up to the level of such powerful technology? Then a kid raised his hand. The audience listened to his question, admired it, and passed it to "Ultronic". The latter remained silent, unable to answer.

"What does it feel like, to be a computer?"

The Internet is more than a knowledge database. It conveys new ways of doing business, of socializing, of finding love. And yet, our Information Age is more than just the Internet.

Let's try to figure this out.

Gold became digital information. We no longer possess gold bars, or gold-convertible bank notes. We pay with credit cards or cell phones. We wire payments from a laptop. The money in a bank account is just a figure on an electronic record, sometimes printed out on a statement. Your total wealth can be physically stored as a few digits on a bank computer's hard drive. Do we have any idea where this mainframe computer is located? And when we think of it, is the value of the computer in the hardware, or in the bank statements it stores?

Just as it was with our international phone call, the value is not in the channel or the support, but in the information. The computer drive of the bank is worth a few thousand dollars, but on it is stored a fortune, millions of dollars worth. Digitalized, but real. Solid gold became information.

Ironically, however, information itself is not yet measured as a value. The amount of intelligence accumulated on the Internet is not quantified in economic terms.

Our fantastical, vertiginous growth of knowledge appears in no GDP, apart from the valuations of big tech firms, as the visible part of the iceberg.

And not only is this huge bulk of knowledge not measured, but its growth is underestimated.

We are facing another exponential effect in knowledge development. How would you call an octopus that can not only build the next rungs of the ladder it climbs, but also develop new artificial arms, and thus climb even faster? An octopus that is able to expand its own capacities, by itself?

Hi there, Artificial Intelligence!

*   *   *

Information Technology is not only about network access, or big data. It is now about self-learning algorithms, commonly called artificial intelligence (AI).

Let us consider how a computer plays a game of chess. It is still not possible for the machine to know all combinations in the game, so the program investigates a few steps ahead, and assesses each situation it reaches with the probability of winning the game. The key, here, is experience: the more the computer plays chess games, the better it adjusts its probability trees. Now, let us imagine that the computer can play against a million players simultaneously instead of just one. Its probability trees (called "heuristics") become very accurate in a very short period of time.

The more the computer plays, the more it improves, without any external help or input other than leveraging the information from lessons learned. Upon winning or losing a game, it updates its statistics to incorporate the game patterns it has encountered. What is most powerful is that the computer enriches its "knowledge" with feedback from reality. This is very close to a self-learning process.

Today, some IT companies promise that, by properly tracking all the information at a plant, it is possible to know when a machine will break down *before* it actually does.

Tomorrow, we will be able to diagnose a cancer before the tumor even appears. Instead of curing diseases, we will prevent them from occurring. Future medicine will be predictive, and this is a major change in healthcare paradigms.

The more the program plays chess, the more it learns. The more data is available, the faster artificial intelligence grows. Yet behind the screen, we still just have computers. They are considerably faster, but mechanically they are roughly the same as the first generation of modern computers (developed in the 1980-90s). Even logically, the basic principles of the underlying code are still "if, then, else". What creates this impression of intelligence is the lesson-learning approach designed into the program. It is the algorithm that enables fast learning. The computer only does what it is good at: computing a large amount of data in a short amount of time. Computers do not know how to do anything else.

Today, a computer would be able to fake an answer for the Penrose kid, in the manner of a smartphone's assistant voice: "I like your question, let me consider it." Or, "I am just a machine you know, I don't really have feelings." Or perhaps, "I feel cool, and you?" Yet, this would still be disguised intelligence. We still have digits processed behind a screen, nothing more. Even if it pretends to, or processes it as information, a computer is not able to feel.

Then, who is controlling this amazing, quick-learning, fast-growing Artificial Intelligence Beast?

More broadly, if humankind were a car, who has the keys? Who's behind the wheel? Who is in charge?

*   *   *

A teenager runs in the Olympic Games. Another is already a drug addict. What is the difference between the two? At a certain point in their lives, each made a decision. Or didn't.

What kind of teenager do we wish humanity to become? How do we consider our choices? How do we decide?

Most elites, whether political, economic, or academic, seem to ignore humanity's amazing growth in population and in knowledge. At best, some try to catch up. A few are gifted at foresight and build business plans out of their vision to start an internet-based company.

What is humankind's business plan? What is our model?

Might we end up in a world of screen-addicted consumers, driven, if not manipulated, by artificial intelligence? A little GAFA* elite village alongside a worldwide slum? Such a risk exists, doesn't it?

---

* Google, Apple, Facebook, Amazon

A founder of a social network has unlimited access to the sensitive data of billions of people. However, he is only holding the leash of a dog that can bark very loudly. As the dog grows bigger and bigger, the leash can no longer hold it back, and the position of power is switched.

The owners of the Internet companies only manage the platform. We still make the conversation.

It is up to our world community to take the power back. To bark louder and take hold of the leash in our teeth. How?

Shall we polarize?

Polarizing is the subtle mechanism that enables a group of elements to generate an image when coordinated together, whereas each is invisible when it is alone. This is surely very rare, isn't it? Actually, it happens billions of times a day. Each time we look at a screen, whether on smartphone, TV or computer, the images we perceive are the result of polarization. LCD, the technology behind the vast majority of these screens, stands for *Liquid Crystal Display*. Well, liquid crystals are invisible in their normal passive state, as they distribute themselves randomly. But if an electrical signal runs through them, they move together, and orient themselves in a coordinated pattern which, once lit, generates an image. A book. A 3D movie. The applications of polarization are incredible.

Essentially, this operates like the schooling instinct of

fish. If they swim together in a coordinated way, they can create the image that will scare away the shark. Fish work together with no electrical signal to coordinate them. They polarize spontaneously.

If fish can do it, why can't we?

*　　*　　*

Otherwise, we will sooner or later face a revolution from those left behind. And, trust my French, no king can stop a revolution.

Yet, you need the likes of a famine to ignite a revolution. And in order to decapitate the king, you need to identify who is wearing the crown. This is not so simple in current times when real power is spread out. Recently, some populist leaders have been fairly adept at faking a famine from five percent unemployment, and faking a king from a disappointing political establishment. But this is no revolution, this is a masquerade. A revolution needs a heart. Populism is just clever manipulation of the crowd by dangerous and foolish people.

A revolution is a dream. Most often unfortunately, it also turns into a bloodbath.

Yet recently, both the Brexit vote and the US election seem to have reflected an underestimated reality: so far, globalization is not an all-winner game.

Surely, the best way to help developing countries is not

just to distribute vaccines or build schools. It is to integrate them into our global economy. But when a plant is relocated from a developed country to a developing one because of lower manufacturing costs, you have two pieces of good news and one piece of bad news: global wealth is better distributed, some people get a job, and others lose theirs.

However, the economic patterns in developed countries are amazingly resilient. It has been decades now since cars, shirts, and even IT services were relocated offshore. Yet the western economy has not collapsed. Furthermore, there are still many areas for improvement or money-wasting to be addressed in our modern countries (a trillion-dollar reckless war in Iraq, for example).

New opportunities appear as quickly as old ones disappear. So why the unease?

Globalization makes some of us feel lost. To be fair, it is not a comfortable period of time. Yes, the challenge for the middle class is tough. Sure, it is not as heart breaking as the Haitian earthquake or the Rwandan genocide, is it? But when you lose your job, you really need a flexible and positive mindset to be able to grab opportunities that are totally different from your previous professional path. Being flexible is becoming an increasingly invaluable skill - and it is not the easiest one to acquire.

We are like passengers in a plane travelling through a

zone of turbulence. Well, how do you handle airsickness, when you're affected by this issue? Either you avoid flying altogether, or, if you must travel for professional reasons, you attend airsickness training. How does this work? There, you are taught *how to fly*. Once you understand how a plane flies and how a pilot operates it, then even though you are still in the passenger cabin the next time, the ability to figure out what is going on makes you feel comfortable with the journey.

To embrace change, we need to understand it.

Unfortunately, it is not an option to get off the globalization plane. We only have one planet, and it is becoming more and more like a village. Unless we apply to become an astronaut on Mars, an interesting yet statistically rare career opportunity, we are bound to accept the globalization trend. But the more we understand it, the easier it will be to handle.

What do you think works better? Embracing change, or fighting against it? The first option opens a world of opportunities. The second is a losing battle.

Now, since there is no pilot in this plane of globalization, we need to polarize to create one, all together.

Humanity is a strange teenager actually. She has no elder brother or sister, and no parent. Except here. All of us. We are both part of this humanity, and parents of the future one. We are educating the humanity who we will hand over to the next generation. We are like a sculpture holding the hammer that is shaping herself.

We are a community of seven billion people that faces the challenges of raising one adolescent humanity. Who do we wish our child to become?

So let us not evade the question any longer, when the answer has become inescapable.

Who is in charge here? We are.

CHAPTER 15

HOW TO DRIVE THE WORLD?

NO GENERATION HAS ever had such a responsibility, or such an opportunity, to influence the destiny of mankind. No generation has ever faced such a challenge.

And yet, how are we doing, in driving our world?

Let's elaborate from recent events, the Brexit referendum and the US presidential elections.

Obviously, both parties that won played on fears. "The world is falling apart, let's protect our island from the rest of the world and try to make the best of it." "Make America Great Again." These are such easy slogans to brandish…

Not only do these recipes not work, but the leaders who trumpet them are pathetic liars. The day after winning the Brexit vote, one abruptly confessed that what he had painted on his campaign bus was plainly false (the £350 million pledged to be put into the British National Health Service), and he cowardly resigned from managing his own political party. Another, even worse, tried to apply what he had promised (the US travel ban executive order), and ended up in a legal mess. So he then invented a story of wiretapping to cover his incompetency with a smokescreen. Is lying the new best practice for running a modern country?

Is something broken in our democracies? Let's have a closer look.

In those two elections with similar stakes, what was perhaps the strongest correlation in the voter groups? That is to say, what was the main driver? Now this is getting a little shocking, so let's have the charts express it, before any comment.

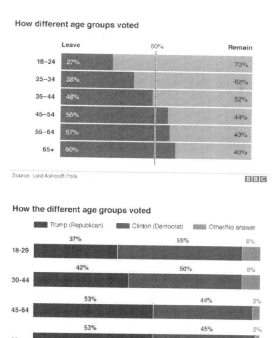

How different age groups voted

How the different age groups voted

Brexit and US presidential elections surveys[57]

Stop this finger-pointing at a middle class afraid of losing their jobs! Middle-class people are used to fighting, and they are much more connected to the world than one would think. Look at the graphs: are people aged six-ty-five and over impacted by the relocation of jobs? The outcome of both elections is not so much related to any economic or social categories.

It is the age factor.

Old people tend to be scared of globalization. Young people tend to embrace it.

The idea is not to step away from one form of finger-pointing and rush to another. But how embarrassing is it to vote *against* this fragile yet beautiful union of countries who had been warring with each other for centuries, and realize the next day that your children and grandchildren voted *for* it, or wished they could have? How inappropriate is it to jeopardize the dream that your children and grand-children strongly believe in? They are already living this dream. They have full year university exchanges in all EU countries. They work abroad as a career opportunity and as a lifestyle. They love this internet-connected, multi-faith, multi-racial environment. This world is their village.

The older ones have stolen the dream from the younger ones. The future belongs to the dreamers and the doers. Not to those who that are scared of it.

The future belongs to our youth.

*   *   *

The key here is to understand that youth is not a matter of age. It is not even a matter of energy, health or humor. It is a mindset.

General Mac Arthur spoke of it beautifully, quoting a poem from Samuel Ullman[58]: "Youth is not a time of life - it is a state of mind. It is not a matter of red cheeks, red lips and supple knees. It is a temper of the will; a quality of the imagination; a vigor of the emotions; it is the freshness of the deep springs of life."

Youth is an attitude.

"Whether seventy or sixteen, there is in every being's heart a love of wonder; the sweet amazement at the stars and starlike things and thoughts; the undaunted challenge of events, the unfailing childlike appetite for what comes next, and the joy in the game of life."

Youth is an invitation. It is still present deep inside each of us.

Let us think again about this expression, a "crisis of growth". The word "crisis" comes from the Greek *krisis*, which means "judgement", "the result of a trial", or "the act of deciding". Amusingly, some would consider a German version of "midlife crisis" to be "*Torschlusspanik*", or "shut-door-panic", meaning "the fear of being on the wrong side of a closing gate".

This is exactly it, isn't it? We all know that globalization, as a force of change, is inevitable. Some of us fear ending up on the wrong side of this new global world. Unfortunately, it is exactly this kind of attitude that leads one into the situation most feared. Fear of the drama drives the drama. The UK and the US are now in much more uneasy positions from which to handle globalization, by having actually voted for Brexit and for a government made up mostly of old, white, male, populist billionaires.

Ironically, while the entire world is required to learn English in order to travel or do business, it is the native speakers of English who seem to be the most afraid of the world! It is no longer an advantage to be an English native speaker. You would be better off learning a second language, and thereby opening your mind. Thus, you become global-agile. You develop flexibility, curiosity, and you get used to thinking differently. You sustain a youthful mindset.

Youth is a philosophy of life that we ought to cherish.

Is this such a terrible challenge?

*   *   *

The Greek language is also the cradle of this great word "democracy", which means: *ruled by the people.* How is democracy doing at a global level?

Here comes the United Nations.

Each time I think of the UN, I recall waiting for my knee surgery at the military hospital and watching a young boy, twenty-years old perhaps, sitting straight-backed in his wheelchair. Both his legs were perforated with external surgical pins. Yet, he so proudly wore his UN peace-keeper T-shirt earned from his activities in the field.

And each time I think of the courage and devotion of the UN peacekeepers, I feel anger towards the UN leaders.

Is there any other organization worldwide that is so incapable of making a decision for five years? How is it that the diplomats of the UN, who are surely brilliant, multilingual, and well paid, have not been able to get any plans approved for Syria since 2011, while its population is being slaughtered by its dictatorial head of state?

Technically, the answer is quite straightforward. *Niet. Niet. Niet. Niet. Niet. Niet. Niet. Niet.*

On eight occasions Russia has exercised its veto power at the UN Security Council (five times coupled with the Chinese delegate), from 2011 to 2017, on whatever resolutions were voted for resolving the Syrian situation[59]. Let's be fair. During the previous decade, the US has played similar games with resolutions on the Israeli-Palestinian conflict (nine vetoes from 2001 to 2006)[60].

The veto rights granted to the five permanent members of the UN Security Council (China, France, Russia, United Kingdom, United States) are the vestige of World War II.

It might have once been legitimate to consider that the five nations who defeated the Nazis could be granted a credit of moral value, which entitles them to such a veto right. However, 300,000 to 500,000 casualties in Syria constitutes a bloodbath that now fully discredits this assumption. It casts shame on the veto holders, and consequently on the UN as well as on the entire international community.

So instead of being democratically represented within an organization of nations, we are kept hostage by it. How do we find a solution to this situation?

Perhaps, we should suggest that our ambassadors to the UN resign. Isn't it shocking that none of them stormed out of the party, finger-pointing at the veto-issuing countries! Or they could try to challenge the veto right at the UN, couldn't they? Request a vote at the UN General Assembly that phases out repetitive veto when they are in collusion with war crimes. Ultimately, start over from scratch with a new international organization, more democratically inclined.

Or perhaps we should just stop banking on the United Nations. Are we not using it as an excuse for our own public opinion silence?

How should the world be ruled, and by whom? Well, shouldn't we start counting on ourselves, since *we are* humanity?

But how could this work? How could might we stand up and walk as one?

How can each of us become an active member of humanity?

Part IV

How to be part of it?

To trust change, we need to understand it. To be confident in the future, we need to feel that we are building it, together.

Consciously raising our future humanity, together, will make each of us grow, become more human and feel more alive.

So, how can we become a part of humankind's current momentum?

CHAPTER 16

FIGURING OUT THE FUTURE

I n 1670 Louis XIV's finance minister, Jean-Baptiste Colbert, initiated a major farming program to cultivate over a million hectares (*2.5 million acres)* of oak trees[61]. This was a strategic move to ensure that, two hundred years later, there would be sufficient wood to build ships for the French Navy. Two hundred years was the time required for the oak trees to reach full maturity and provide the lumber needed for ship construction.

Less than three centuries later, France was freed from the Nazi occupation thanks to the greatest navy operation ever organized, the Normandy landing. But only 177 French soldiers were involved* (the Kieffer Commandos, on the front line), out of a total of 156,000 from thirteen

---

* The French Army was actually focused on the South-East France Landing (August 1944). There, 200,000 French soldiers fought, out of a total of 450,000 Allied soldiers.

allied countries on D-day[62]. Ironically, France's century-long enemy, the United Kingdom, had become one of its greatest allies. And yet, four years earlier (July 3rd, 1940), the British Navy "accidentally" sank a full squadron of French ships peacefully anchored in North Africa (Mers-el-Kebir, 1,297 French fatalities)[63].

Even though the conflict itself, the complexity of its progression, and the combination of alliances were far beyond the imagination of any seventeenth-century leader, Colbert had accurately anticipated that the Navy would be a major stake in the long term.

But none of the military ships in WWII were made of oak.

Nevertheless, forests are important assets today to counter global warming and protect biodiversity. And France is the world's number one tourist destination thanks, in part, to how well its coasts and countryside are preserved. Such attention to nature directly stems from Colbert's strategic initiative with the oak trees.

With a similar mindset, Napoleon, whose artillery-calculating skills had been key to winning his battles, created the *Ecole Polytechnique*, a selective university dedicated to nurturing mathematically-gifted officers for the French Army. Two hundred years later, very few *Polytechnique* graduates actually embark on a military career. But the presence of this elite engineering school and of the other so-called "Grandes Ecoles" has enabled France to develop world industry leaders in most areas of engineering: automotive, aeronautics, space, energy, materials, life sciences, food products, cosmetics, pharmaceuticals, chemistry, and others.

Colbert and Napoleon's predictions were not so accurate. But the outcomes of their forward-thinking turned out to be most relevant. Furthermore, Napoleon's underlying key attitude in strategic thinking was to "expect the unexpected." Think *beyond* what can be planned.

Even though France benefited from some visionary leaders like Napoleon and Colbert, who were able to think so far ahead, until recently the country's common view of globalization was a deeply negative one: "*Tout fout le camp!*" would people often say. "Everything is falling apart!"*

In spite of the Mers-el-Kebir tragedy, or perhaps because of it, Churchill became the biggest supporter for France to be granted the fifth seat as permanent member of the UN Security Council, with power to veto. Unfortunately, half a century later, neither the UK nor the US listened to France's recommendation regarding the second Iraqi war. In a nutshell, this French position was that it is one thing to win a war, but it is another thing to win peace afterwards.

---

* The recent 2017 presidential elections in France seem to convey a surge of optimism: great news!

As it turned out, no plans had been drawn up to manage the "postwar" period in Iraq. That void led to the destabilization of the entire area, and to the rise of ISIS.

Planning might lead to some mistakes. No planning at all will invariably result in the worst possible scenario.

On that note, if we were asked to name a leader today who thinks 200 years ahead, who could we point to?

Do we have a leader on the world stage able to think even five decades ahead?

Does any head of state think much beyond the next election?

*   *   *

Some plans were put in place, relatively recently. In September 2000, following a series of international meetings and conferences, the UN General Assembly adopted a resolution called the "UN Millennium Declaration", which defined eight "Millennium Goals". It aimed to reduce extreme poverty, to promote primary education, and so on. Related targets were to be achieved by 2015. Then, a new set of seventeen "sustainable development goals" was launched[64]. Ever heard of them? Were the previous eight achieved[65]?

Let's not be too hard on the United Nations. Its annual budget amounts to only three billion USD (not including external peace keeping operations, which are funded by another seven billion USD). The Bill & Melinda Gates foundation has a similar "budget"*. Yes, a two-person philanthropic initiative has roughly the same annual budget as an official supranational organization supported by almost all countries on the planet. This represents 0.2% of estimated global military spending (1,700 billion USD[66] per year).

It's a ratio of one to 170 between peace-keeping and military expenses.

With so little investment, the UN does what it can. Let's not shoot at the ambulance, even though it may be wobbly. But why is the UN not better supported and more decently funded?

The issue is that, at the national level, our future has been kidnapped by political leaders who use globalization as a scapegoat for their lack of achievement. Not only is this reflective of incompetence, but it also opens the door to populist leaders, who become elected by selling the past as a future. "Make America Great Again" literally translates as: "Let's go back to the way things were." Protectionism is a personality trait posing as policy, one that can be summarized in two words: Me first!

Besides, in our beautiful democracies, when a head of state by-passes international organizations and

---

* Bill & Melinda Gates Foundation's annual grantee support: four billion USD.

ignores international laws in order to launch a baseless 125,000-fatality war[*], he walks away from it without any trial - possibly without even being questioned! A driver who causes an accident by ignoring a red light ends up in far more trouble.

So what we currently have, in our integrated and globalized world, is a number of political leaders who lack international experience and are not really accountable to anyone; a disappointing international central organization, the UN, granted with a tiny budget; and massive weapons industries, not to mention other major economic forces, that are simply pursuing profit. And all of them have "long-term" objectives set for five to fifteen years ahead, at the most.

Is there anyone else around to provide a plan?

Really, no hands up? Are we in such a desert, when it comes to promoting a vision, imagining our future, sharing a dream?

Where will we be 200 years from now?

*   *   *

What is striking is not only the absence of a plan, but the lack of awareness regarding the challenge we are up against.

---

[*] 2003-11 Iraq war estimated fatalities: 100,000 civilians, 20,000 Iraqi soldiers, 5,000 coalition soldiers.

Have we ever been presented with the amazing growth that humanity is currently experiencing?

And where does this leave us? We are in charge, with no map, no target, and no leaders.

What is the solution? To be careful in our individual choices and to maximize the polarization effect? To vote thoughtfully, whenever we are asked to, as potential kingmakers?

I am not a global decision-maker, so apart from sorting out the bins, clicking on news, and carrying out my civil duties, what can I do?

I wish to be part of it. I understand that global changes require me to sustain a young and agile mindset. I accept that the journey is likely to be uncomfortable.

What's next? How can I become a part of what is currently going on?

Is there a purpose for me in this world?

CHAPTER 17

WHAT ELSE BUT FATE?

THIS QUESTION IS 3,000 years old. The book of Ecclesiastes in the Bible, among the most ancient texts in human history, begins with this statement: "Vanity of vanities, all is vanity," which can be translated as "all is to no purpose." Surprisingly, a few lines later comes the following: "he who increases in knowledge also increases in sorrow."

Is it that different today? Have we progressed beyond these assessments? Let's give it some thought. The Internet revolution has allowed us to make incredible leaps in accumulating knowledge, but has this brought us anything other than sorrow? Is there any purpose to all of these technologies? When it comes to the World Wide Web, smartphones, social networks, big data, artificial intelligence, and all the connected objects we can buy: truly, are they nothing but "vanities"?

In the twenty-first century, hasn't life become like a big supermarket in which we just shop around?

What else but fate? Considering that we are facing a "crisis of growth", if we leverage the meaning of "crisis" as an "opportunity to decide", then how we answer this question is up to each of us.

It's probably more comfortable to take the easy route. Pretend to be a citizen of the world. Allow ourselves twenty minutes a day to catch up on the news. Empathize with the sorrows of the world, then switch off, and enjoy our own little island of happiness.

Or push it a little further, and become skeptical, or cynical, about watching the world without being able to do anything about it.

Or we can even disconnect completely, and just enjoy life with its daily distractions.

"All these are toys, in the end" explained an uncle of mine. "I'm forty-five years old, but I still play with toys, just like a kid." He was talking of his nice watch, his powerful four wheel drive car, and his beautiful sailing yacht. The cancer he was fighting had obviously made him reconsider a few things. Two years before, he had been about to cross the Atlantic with a crew of friends, when he was informed of the disease. He had surgery, underwent an initial round of chemotherapy, and then set off on the ocean with his friends. Onboard was the second injection of chemo drugs, ready to be taken if the journey lasted too long. And that's how he fulfilled his dream of sailing the Atlantic Ocean. His will defeated his fate.

Does it take a crisis like cancer to make us think of our lives? To reject fate? To make our own choices?

We are at a critical moment of transition in the evolution of humankind. Do we wish to sit on the sidelines and ignore it?

Should we be a spectator, a consumer? Or a little cell, part of humanity, providing our small but unique contribution that is important for the whole body to function?

What is the alternative? How do we escape from fatalism? Where is there an Atlantic ocean to cross, a challenge to embark on, a new dream to embrace?

* * *

All the ways of man are to no purpose. This is a shocking statement. Or perhaps it calls for a question: is it really so? Ecclesiastes eventually concludes:

> "Respect God and keep his commandments, for this is the whole duty of man."

In other words, our destiny is in God's hands, and it is beyond our level of understanding.

Twenty-eight centuries later, in the Age of Enlightenment,

Voltaire provided a philosophical answer in his novel, *Candide*. The hero grows through a series of hurdles and disenchantments in his life. Finally he finds his way, and enigmatically states, "We must cultivate our garden."

Whether religious or philosophical, these conclusions are similar: searching for a meaning in our lives or in the world is pointless. We can only try to do our best each day, and forget about futile dreams. This is also close to the concept of karma in Asia, isn't it? Whether from God, from fate, or from reincarnation, doing our best in the little things means we shall be rewarded eventually. In practical terms, if we wish to have an impact on global warming, the best we can do is to properly sort out our rubbish. Small acts from individuals will contribute to the good of our world, and to humankind.

What about the other statement? Does an increase in knowledge really lead to an increase in sorrow? Maybe. But what if I wish to better understand, to become part of something bigger than my own destiny?

Most likely, such a quest will be in vain. In his essay *The Hunger of the Tiger,*[67] René Barjavel writes that man might be like a tiger in a cage from which it is impossible to escape, with a hunger for a knowledge that is out of his reach. But then, explains the author, he'd rather be a tiger that stands and paces, even round and round inside the cage, than a tiger that sleeps.

Most of us will accept fate. Some of us will even have a positive attitude about it, which surely is close to wisdom. Yet, what about becoming a bird and flying beyond the bars of resignation?

A man once became trapped in the most terrible cage imaginable, the cruelest prison: his own body. One night, driving back home with his son, he felt dizzy, stopped the car, and fainted. He woke up in a hospital, with locked-in syndrome, suffering from ninety-nine percent paralysis. He was left with the ability to move only one eyelid - not even both. He could hear his friends speaking loudly, by his bed, about how tragic it was for him to have become a vegetable. A physiologist noticed that the eyelid was moving and she approached him. She developed a way of communicating. She pointed out letters on a board, and as she read through them she paid attention to when his eyelid shut. This process enabled the man with locked-in syndrome to write a book. A touching, award-winning book that became a bestseller, and from which a Golden Globe-winning movie was produced. From his body-prison, by simply moving his left eyelid, Jean-Dominique Bauby wrote *The Diving Bell and The Butterfly*[68].

If a man so severely handicapped is able to write a 140-page beautiful book, then is it so much out of our reach to break open the cage of fatalism in which we are trapped, and figure out our common destiny as one humanity?

*   *   *

Where is today my "garden" to be cultivated? Is it in social networks? Strangely, these enable us to stay in touch easily with friends far away, yet the time we spend on screens distances us from friends close by. We may feel connected with events taking place thousands of miles away, but would we still have a beer with a stranger at the pub down the block?

Barjavel shares another powerful image. He says we are like the cells of the leg of an athlete that runs, yet we might never to know the athlete's destination, nor even that we are part of her leg.

Let's explore this image. Think of men and women as the cells of a large body, a living entity called humanity. What do we know about this entity, apart from the fact that it is experiencing an amazing crisis of growth? Should humanity be compared to an athlete, or to a plankton cloud?

There are clues that we, "cells", try to gather. We have the United Nations, and many international organizations, trying to help throughout the world. We have global information, businesses, tourism. And we have public opinion that sometimes speaks with a single voice.

Are we walking somewhere? If we are, then surely we must be running, because the acceleration of time seems vertiginous.

And if we are running, a scary question arises: *where* are we running to?

No figures can answer such a question. We can measure how quickly we are growing, and potentially even how fast we are running. But how can we learn of our destination?

Let's go back to the original meaning of the word *crisis,* in Greek: the act of deciding.

What is the only difference between the teenager who runs races and the one who takes drugs? The decision each one once made. So the answer is actually crystal clear.

We are running to where we will decide to run.

CHAPTER 18

WHERE ARE WE RUNNING TO?

S O WE WILL run to wherever we decide. Now what?

How will this play out? We have no leader in charge of "humankind" as a whole, only a limited organization in the form of the United Nations, which is currently attempting to achieve seventeen goals unknown to most people.

But this also creates an opportunity. *We* are in charge of our own destiny. *We* are the ones who must answer this question. We might be like fish in the ocean that school together, guided by no master or political organization. But some species of fish naturally collaborate, together as one team. What is their secret?

Perhaps fish just do it instinctively to survive, without

thinking. Perhaps they just swim within the group, and the group happens to swim somewhere. What other examples of natural group synchronization can we think of?

What about public applause? At the end of a play or concert, when an audience rejoices, many individuals naturally synchronize and clap together. And here we have hundreds or thousands of people who catch the rhythm and, within a few seconds, are able to follow it. To understand just how exceptional this is, one could ask any army instructor how long it takes to train a troop of thirty soldiers to walk in step with one another. This requires a few hours, compared to a few seconds of applause in the theater. Certainly, it is more difficult to march than to simply clap. Yet, in both cases, the trick is in the listening. Once people *get it*, they immediately synchronize with each other.

What would we need, as "cells of humanity", to become coordinated? A common goal? A vision?

We need a feeling. We need an emotion. We need a dream.

*   *   *

It is not possible to read the word "dream" without thinking of the most powerful speech of the twentieth century. This speech was actually improvised, even though its author surely nurtured it inwardly long before. On August 28th, 1963, at the Lincoln Memorial in Washington DC, Martin Luther King preached to a large gathering.

As he finished, his friend Mahalia Jackson shouted from the crowd: "Tell us about your dream!" Then he spoke, straight from his heart, the simple words that have since moved billions of people[69].

"I have a dream that one day [...] little black boys and black girls will be able to join hands with little white boys and white girls as sisters and brothers."

Martin Luther King had a generous vision for us, in which we all have a place.

And yet, it wasn't enough, was it? Decades later, Barack Obama was elected the first African-American President of the US, opening a new era of hope. A commentator confidently expressed that he would be "the first and the last", in that the ethnicity of the next African-American president in the future would simply go unnoticed. Yet when Obama completed his second term in 2016, discrimination seemed to be stronger than it had ever been in the previous decades in the US.

With all due respect to Martin Luther King, and with much admiration for his charisma, his message and his legacy, there might be something missing from his dream: the identity on which it is based. This thought struck me while I was talking with a group of international friends in Europe. During the conversation, I made a passing reference to "the black community". An American woman immediately corrected this into what she deemed the more politically correct "African-American". Some of us smiled. In France, the community descended from Africa would not describe themselves as such. In fact, they prefer the English word, "black". They find it more than cool. The word is somehow "chic" in its succinctness and in the way it sounds. "Chic" is a magic word in French, it means: nice, elegant, trendy. So, in French, the English word "black" is "chic". Now, what if, in American English, we could happily state: "Black is chic!"

A dream is a vision that you believe in, that you can contribute to and that takes root in your identity.

Do we share an identity as "one humanity"?

*　　*　　*

Back to the previous example of the theater: why does the crowd so rapidly synchronize when applauding? Together, they just experienced something special. For a couple of hours, they shared feelings: happiness, sadness, love, awe, drama and beauty. Whatever the performers expressed on stage was so strong that by the end of the show the crowd had united.

We are running to wherever we decide to run. Why does a vision not arise? Why do dreams go unheard? Surely, some have dreams here and there. Why are they unnoticed and overwhelmed by pessimism?

Let us look at a teenager who runs.

Do we have any idea about where this young woman is running to? No. Yet, there is something powerful in this picture. She is obviously happy to run.

It is the feeling that we lack. We need to *feel* that we are, together, "one humanity", growing and running. We sweat. Sometimes it aches. Sometimes it gets easier. Sometimes it's just great. It might rain along the way. There might be beautiful scenery after the next bend in the path.

Here we are, standing up, moving forward. We are running! Feel it!

Right now, think of all the people across the world. Waking up and hoping to have a nice day. Shaking hands.

Sharing a lunch. Working hard. Relaxing. Socializing. Sleeping. Each with our own goals. Each waiting for a common dream to share.

Sense that we are all on one planet, interconnected by the rhythm of our days and nights. Feel that we are one body made of "human beings" that are "cells of humankind".

Breathe! Sense that we are running as one humanity, just like this young woman in the picture.

- But where to?

CHAPTER 19

AN ANSWER HIDING IN THE QUESTION

THE ANSWER IS pretty simple: we don't know yet.

However, it's subtler than that. The answer lies within the question.

Rainer Maria Rilke phrased it beautifully in his *Letters to a Young Poet*[70], suggesting that some questions are meant to be enjoyed for themselves:

> "Live the questions now. Perhaps then, someday far in the future, you will gradually, without even noticing it, live your way into the answer."

We don't know yet where we are running to. The answer will emerge along the way. Our young woman in the picture might not know yet where she is running, but she is happy to run. She *feels* it.

All we need is an identity, a feeling, a soul. The dream, the vision, the destination will emerge as we progress.

Yet, all runners know that every step, every run, is a victory. We could easily stay at home. We can also stay divided, pursuing our own selfish ambitions, treasuring our comfortable little islands. Then we would be regressing.

Our teenage adolescent humanity has not yet consciously decided between aiming for an Olympic medal, building a healthy and balanced life, or becoming embroiled in drugs.

What I am aiming for in life? This question has no definite answer. It actually works in the same way that a compass helps a sailor. When you look at it, it enables you to set a direction, which will be readjusted further on. Isn't this how each of us progress in life? We try to do the best we can. We have goals, some of which we meet and some we don't. We grow from our successes, and even more from our failures. We mature. We fine-tune the course of our lives accordingly.

Where are we heading? "Live the question now" means a few different things. Firstly, the answer will not come all at once. It is more like completing a puzzle, for which we receive a few new pieces each day. It's like a sculpture that gradually takes shape under the tools of its creator. It is like a book being written.

It also means that the question contains its own mystery. The answer comes from regularly reflecting on the question. What about "live" it? This means that the question is enjoyable, that it makes us move forward. It makes us grow. "Where am I running to?" is an invitation to go further.

Life is not an equation to resolve. It is a mystery to explore.

So is humanity.

$$* \quad * \quad *$$

If the answer is a process, and not a solution, then how can we best answer the question: *where are we running?*

This is a four-word question. There is a destination, *"where"*, and a momentum, *"are running"*. What about the *we*?

We are. *I am.* The building block is our identity.

How should I define myself? Through my current job? Through my origins? Through my childhood dreams? Let's play around with words a little. Basic words, such as "dad", "mom", "yes", "no", often sound similar in languages that are culturally close. Mom, *Mama* (German), *Maman* (French). No, *nein, non.* Yes, *ja, oui.* Yes in French, *"oui"*, sounds exactly like "we" in English.

What if, in the middle of the question, we hear a "yes": *where are "oui" running?*

What if "we" had a profoundly positive meaning behind it? A "we/yes", so to speak.

If humanity were an image being painted, where would I be? Holding the paintbrush? Part of the paint? A detail in the image? Or a spectator, watching the creation? Pablo Picasso, among other artists, believed that a painting "lives" only in the eye of the beholder. The observer is co-creator of the painting. What if our main responsibility is to look *positively* at the growth of humanity?

How would this work if we were really talking about a teenager? Any parent probably knows this trick. If you tell a child *not* to do something, the child will likely do it. Whereas if you encourage him or her in a good initiative, the child will often pursue it. It is the eye on the child that best shapes the child. If such an eye is positive, the child will progress, gain self-confidence, and make wise choices. His or her own choices.

Could our eye on the world actually change the world? Surely.

Where are we running? If we choose to have a positive vision on this question, we are already encouraging humanity to grow, and run.

*   *   *

Unfortunately, the opposite works as well. If pessimism, protectionism and selfishness keep mushrooming, then mankind is likely to halt, or perhaps even regress.

We are facing a beautiful opportunity, but whether we take it or not is undecided.

Perhaps this is similar in some ways to a team-building exercise. How do such training sessions work? Several individuals are placed in front of a challenge that cannot be achieved by each one alone. They will need to help each other to win. They will need to combine their strengths. Imagine ants facing an obstacle a few inches tall: by climbing on each other, then pulling one another, they can overcome the obstacle. Are we humans able to do the same? When assembled as a team, with dedicated training, we can succeed, and thereby feel closer to our partners. Team spirit arises from a common endeavor. Should we come up with a team-building exercise for the whole of humankind?

In fact, this is how the League of Nations was created, after the First World War. It is also how the United Nations organization came into existence, after World War II. A global feeling of horror at so many deaths led to establishing these international organizations dedicated to defusing future conflicts among nations. Could we please avoid a third world war, and start to understand what is preventing such organizations from becoming more efficient? It is not the politics that makes the team, but the team spirit. To become a team, we first need to share *the feeling* of being a team.

The soul of Humanity needs to be awakened.

Let's cast a compassionate eye on ourselves, and start enjoying this enlivening question: "Where are we running?"

This is how we will nurture a global soul.

This is how we might, one day, make the decision together to run for the gold.

CHAPTER 20

A NEW STAGE FOR HUMANITY

S OME TEENAGERS ARE balanced and happy. Others struggle. All eventually grow. Humanity will experience growth, regardless. Teenagers eventually become adults.

But humanity is not just facing a crisis of growth. We are about to take a new step in our development.

One man predicted this almost a century ago: Mr. Pierre Teilhard de Chardin[71]. He was a brilliant biologist. He was also a priest, yet one able to think very much outside of the box of the Catholic Church's official positions on science. A man ahead of his time, Teilhard respected both Darwin and the Bible, for he considered both to be true explanations of humankind from two complementary angles. His outstanding scientific rigor enabled him to anticipate both current globalization and a theory recently published in 2010 as the *Last Universal Common Ancestor*.

In a nutshell, Teilhard considered the beginning of life on Earth as an exceptional quantum leap, which most likely occurred in a single event on the planet. A molecule unexpectedly became a living cell, and we all descend from this cell. With another leap came our thinking processes. To have thoughts - consciousness - coming from living cells is as scientifically mysterious as to have life surging from inert matter. In the twenty-first century, we are able to clone animals, yet we still have no clue how to instigate these two technological leaps: to create life from inert organic material, and to generate thoughts from biological tissues.

What is fascinating in his theory, and somehow thrilling, is what comes next. According to Teilhard de Chardin, we still have one more quantum leap to make. This is when all individual consciences will converge into one global spirit. Decades before the arrival of the Internet and of social networks, and at the beginning of humankind's crisis of growth, Teilhard was predicting the emergence of a "collective human soul".

And this is happening *right now*.

*　　*　　*

Unless a military dictatorship arises and commands us

to march in step through the streets, we will still make our own ways as usual. In other words, we are not going to aggregate into a giant molecule. Each of us is still a free human being. The idea is that, like the phenomenon called "public opinion", we shall begin to synchronize more and more naturally, as part of this all-encompassing "soul" of humanity.

The good news is that this will inevitably happen. In fact, it is already happening as global trends attest. The bad news is that we are not aware of it. We are like a teen-ager with no elder sibling to show us the way. We are the first to ever experience this. Just like adolescence, it is a transition phase and a step forward. It can be quite enjoyable. It can also turn into an uncomfortable, scary, and depressing period.

And like an adolescent, if we do not sense a positive eye upon us, we are likely to stray off course.

Actually, it's not about whether to run for the Olympics or not. A gold medal is just a piece of metal. Whether the competitor wins it or not is a mere detail. What matters is how he or she trained for it, and became an athlete.

It is all in the attitude. Live your dream of sailing even when set back by cancer. Write a book using only one eyelid while ninety-nine percent paralyzed. And for most of us, simply try to do our best.

Yet, as the Greek word *"krisis"* reminds us, each of us

faces an important choice in this defining moment of our human history. A one-word decision.

Trust.

Shall we trust humanity? Will we trust our future? Do we wish to trust one another?

Shall I trust myself?

* * *

Trust is not the outcome of analyzing whether or not our complex world is heading in the right direction. Trust is the prerequisite. Trust is a choice.

Trust is actually *the* choice, that will allow us to grow together, or else drift apart.

What if, right now, in a silent revolution, we decide to come together and to believe again in ourselves?

What if we start to think, and *feel*, that each one of us is a worthy cell in the body of humanity?

Like a smile, perhaps. Smiling sometimes requires a little effort - but not so much. A smile doesn't seem to change anything, but it changes your whole day. It can change a life.

Let's remember the spark that we mentioned a little while ago, the spark to be cast on the world. What if we looked a little closer at one another, and tried to find this spark in each other's eyes? And be "sparked" in return. Then the spark becomes a seed.

Wouldn't you like to be a seed?

It is not easy, as time flies and life goes on, to keep trusting each other, and to maintain faith in the future. Faith in oneself is sometimes even the hardest.

But trust is an invitation to live.

Feel, and trust, that we are part of something bigger. Perhaps, Humanity is the dream of God. Perhaps this world is just an extraordinary coincidence of chance. In either case, it is up to us to build our world, isn't it? It is up to us to grow as one Humanity.

We are the Figures of Mankind.

CONCLUSION

F IGURES ALLOW US to better understand our world. As mankind, we are currently doing well, surprisingly well. We are experiencing a momentum, a crisis of growth, unique in our whole 5,500-year human history. Like an adolescent, we are undergoing significant progress including changes that we do not yet fully understand. We are also enduring some discomfort and pain. We have doubts about where we are heading, where we are and who we are.

When I run, I feel self-confidence in my own way. I feel that I am advancing, that I am running towards something in my life, even though the destination is still unclear. I enjoy myself. In fact, I just feel good! Shouldn't we feel the same way, as one Humanity that runs?

In the previous pages, we explored a few figures which enabled us to better picture our world, to properly "figure it out". But what finally emerges is more than a pun. *We are* the figures of mankind. And we are collectively responsible for the future of Humanity. Let's look forward, and smile at the journey ahead.

The challenge of our current generation is to unite as one and become aware that we are growing so tremendously, not only in population, but also in knowledge. As with adolescence, this is happening before we are mature enough to deal with it. We will mature. Or perhaps, we won't. This is what is at stake. Our calling is to awaken humanity's consciousness as a common soul and grow together.

Where are we running to? The answer is incubating in the question. We are running to where we will decide to go, which is still out of reach as a choice. Yet today, we must take ownership of our own destiny, and together imagine who we wish to become as one Humanity.

As the poet Rainer Maria Rilke invites us to observe, the key is not so much to look for an answer, but to take time to consider the question. Think of it. Love it.

Whenever one of us starts enjoying the question of our common destiny, we, Humanity, take a little step forward. Once all of us do, then we shall become this athlete, self-confidently running towards a dream we will shape along the way.

Please don't wait for the others to start first. Take this

step. Your step. Be just a little more than who you think you are. Not just a human being. Become a "co-creating human being". A cell of our common humanity that is just starting to stand up, walk, and run.

Actually, we have already experienced some major periods of progress. There was the "Enlightenment Century" in the 1700s. Shortly after was the Industrial Revolution by the 1800s. These were times of social, political and scientific advancements, combined with hope and enthusiasm. Then came the dreadful World Wars which might have locked humanity into pessimism.

It is time to wake up.

Together, let us ignite the spark that will launch the Century of the New Enlightenment.

Together, let's put our jogging shoes on and enthusiastically run forward as one Humanity.

ACKNOWLEDGEMENTS

To write a book is a long road to run. This would not have been possible without the supportive help of a few friends, either in challenging my text or my ideas, or just in sharing some enthusiasm for this project.

I would like to warmly thank Kristen, Nathalie, Micheline Rollin, Martin Slack, Yves, Debra Moffitt, Susannah, Colette, Tom, Jean-François, Vlassis Tigkarakis, Nicolas, Jean, and of course Erwan, as well as all those who inspired me to craft a fairly optimistic mindset, whatever the weather.

ENDNOTES

1   USGS Earthquake Hazards Program, Earthquake
     Facts
     (https://earthquake.usgs.gov/learn/facts.php)

2   France Television, JT 20 heures, January 13, 2010
     (www.youtube.com/watch?v=B-0lq559r4Q);
     Le Figaro, le Premier Ministre Haïtien craint plus de
     100,000 morts, January13, 2010
     (www.lefigaro.fr/internation-
     al/2010/01/13/01003-20100113ARTFIG00373-hai-
     ti-ravage-par-un-violent-seisme-.php)
     The New York Daily News, Haiti Government Calls
     Off Search and Rescue Effort, January 24, 2010
     (www.nydailynews.com/news/world/haiti-govern-
     ment-calls-search-rescue-effort-united-nations-arti-
     cle-1.458584)

3   WHO Unicef, Water and Sanitation Use in Haïti,
     June 2015
     (https://washdata.org/data#!/hti)

4   CNCD, Haiti : l'Echec Humanitaire, January 18,

2013
(www.cncd.be/Haiti-l-echec-humanitaire)

5   NBC News, Fukushima Evacuation Has Killed
     more than Earthquake and Tsunami, survey says,
     September 10, 2013
     (https://www.nbcnews.com/news/other/fukushima-
     evacuation-has-killed-more-earthquake-tsunami-sur-
     vey-says-f8C11120007)

6   Le Monde, Plus de 400 Morts dans les Inondations
     en Inde et au Pakistan, September 09, 2014
     (http://www.lemonde.fr/planete/article/2014/09/09/
     plus-de-400-morts-dans-les-inondations-en-inde-et-
     au-pakistan_4484522_3244.html)

7   USGS, Indian Ocean Tsunami Remembered,
     December 23, 2014
     (www.usgs.gov/news/indian-ocean-tsuna-
     mi-remembered-scientists-reflect-2004-in-
     dian-ocean-killed-thousands)

8   Libération, Bilan des Victimes, l'Impos-
     sible Comptage, March 10, 2016 (www.
     liberation.fr/planete/2016/03/10/
     bilan-des-victimes-l-impossible-comptage_1438845)

9   CNN, September 11 Anniversary Fast Facts, updated
     August 24, 2017
     (http://edition.cnn.com/2013/07/27/us/
     september-11-anniversary-fast-facts/)

10   The New York Post, FDNY at pre-9/11 numbers,
      December 12, 2003
      (https://nypost.com/2003/12/12/
      fdny-at-pre-911-numbers/)

11   icasualty.org, Iraq and Afghanistan Coalition Military
      Fatalities by year, 2001-2017
      (http://icasualties.org)

12   French Ministry of Defense, Operation Pamir (2001-
      2014), In Memoriam
      (www.defense.gouv.fr/operations/opera-
      tions/autres-operations/operations-achevees/
      operation-pamir-2001-2014/in-memoriam/
      in-memoriam)

13   Congressional Research Service, Iraqi Civilian Deaths
      Estimates, RS22537, August 27, 2008
      (www.everycrsreport.com/files/20061122_RS22537_
      a3a2ff7d7efe6af2a1111632ba016cc6eec9a9bc.pdf)

14   The New York Times, The 2004 campaign: the
      former vice-president Gore Says Bush Betrayed the
      U.S. by Using 9/11 as a Reason for War in Iraq;
      February 09, 2004
      (www.nytimes.com/2004/02/09/us/2004-campaign-
      former-vice-president-gore-says-bush-betrayed-us-us-
      ing-9-11-reason.html)

15   Former Vice President Al Gore, Iraq and the War on
      Terrorism (Commonwealth Club of California , San

Francisco, California), September 23, 2002
(http://p2004.org/gore/gore092302sp.html)

16   Federal Election Commission, 2000 Official
      Presidential General Election Results
      (https://transition.fec.gov/pubrec/2000presgeresults.htm)

17   United Nations International Court Tribunal for
      the former Yugoslavia, Death Toll in the Siege of
      Sarajevo, April 1992 to December 1995, Expert
      report prepared for the Case of Slobodan Milo(evi),
      Bosnia and Herzegovina, August 18, 2003
      (www.icty.org/x/file/About/OTP/War_
      Demographics/en/slobodan_milosevic_sara-
      jevo_030818.pdf)

18   Paul Garde, Vie et mort de la Yougoslavie (Fayard,
      1992)

19   Tribune de Genève, Les Quatre Ans d'un Conflit
      Meurtrier, April 05, 2012
      (www.tdg.ch/monde/europe/Les-
      quatre-ans-d-un-conflit-meurtrier/
      story/23018988)

20   International Center for Transitional Justice, Former
      Yugoslavia Fact Sheets, 2009
      (www.ictj.org/sites/default/files/ICTJ-
      FormerYugoslavia-Justice-Facts-2009-English.pdf)

21   United Nations department of Public Information,

Outreach Program on the Rwanda Genocide and the United Nations, (www.un.org/en/preventgenocide/rwanda/education/ rwandagenocide.shtml)

22 P.Watzlawick, J.Weakland, R.Fisch, Change: Principles of Problem Formation & Problem Resolution (W. W. Norton & Company, 1974) and P.Watzlawick, The Language of Change (W. W. Norton & Company, 1977)

23 United Nations, Economic and Social Affairs, World Population prospects: 2017 & 2012 revisions, Key Findings and Advance Tables (https://esa.un.org/unpd/wpp/Publications)

24 ATD Fourth World, FAQ: How many people living in poverty are there? (www.atd-fourthworld.org/who-we-are/faq/)

25 United Nations, Economic and Social Affairs, Report

on the world situation 2010 (p14)
(www.un.org/esa/socdev/rwss/docs/2010/fullreport.pdf)

26   Les Echos, Des chiffres de plus en plus déconnectés de la réalité, Feb 26, 2018 (www.lesechos.fr/idees-debats/editos-analyses/0301347003578-des-chiffres-de-plus-en-plus-de-connectes-de-la-realite-2156610.php)

27   CNEWS Matin, Les Accidents de Car les plus Meurtriers en Europe, July 29, 2013 (www.cnewsmatin.fr/monde/2013-07-29/les-accidents-de-car-les-plus-meurtriers-en-europe-519740)

28   United Nations, Economic and Social Affairs, Population and Vital Statistics Report, January 2017 (https://unstats.un.org/unsd/demographic-social/products/vitstats/sets/Series_A_2017.pdf)

29   The Telegraph, The Holocaust Death Toll, January 26, 2005,(www.telegraph.co.uk/news/1481975/The-Holocaust-death-toll.html)

30   The Guardian, Jewish Global Population Approaches pre-Holocaust Levels, January 28, 2015(www.theguardian.com/world/2015/jun/28/jewish-global-population-approaches-pre-holocaust-levels)

31   The New York Times, Armenian Genocide of 1915: an Overview(www.nytimes.com/ref/timestopics/topics_armeniangenocide.html)

32 UCLA Newsroom, UCLA demographer produces best estimate yet of Cambodia's death toll under Pol Pot, April 16, 2015(http://newsroom.ucla.edu/releases/ucla-demographer-produces-best-estimate-yet-of-cambodias-death-toll-under-pol-pot)

33 Encyclopaedia Britannica, World War I, Killed, Wounded and Missing(www.britannica.com/event/World-War-I/Killed-wounded-and-missing)

34 United Nations, The World at Six Billion, October 1999(www.un.org/esa/population/publications/sixbillion/sixbilpart1.pdf)

35 BBC, Iraq War in Figures, December 14, 2001, (www.bbc.com/news/world-middle-east-11107739) and previously mentioned sources (icasualty, Encyclopaedia Britannica, UN World at Six Billions)

War Yearly Fatality rates	Casualties	Related Population	Period	Duration (in year)	Yearly Fatality Rate
Iraqi war (Coalition soldiers)	4,852	110,000	2003-11	9	0.5%
WW1 (soldiers)	8,528,831	65,038,810	1914-18	4	3.3%

36 Encyclopaedia Britannica, World War II, Cost of the War, Killed, Wounded and Missing

(www.britannica.com/event/World-War-II/
Hiroshima-and-Nagasaki#ref53607)

37   United Nations, The World at Six Billion,
      October 1999

38   World Health Organization, Media Center,
      Preventing Unsafe Abortion
      (www.who.int/mediacentre/factsheets/fs388/en/)

39   United Nations, Economic and Social Affairs,
      Population Division, World Abortion Policies, 2013
      (www.un.org/en/development/desa/population/publi-
      cations/policy/world-abortion-policies-2013.shtml)

40   Guttmacher Institute, Fact sheet, Induced Abortion
      Worldwide, May 2016,
      (www.guttmacher.org/fact-sheet/induced-abor-
      tion-worldwide)
      United Nations, Economic and Social Affairs,
      Population Division, World Population Prospect
      (2017), Births / Fertility
      (https://esa.un.org/unpd/wpp/Download/Standard/
      Fertility)
      Insee, T65 - Évolution du nombre des interrup-
      tions volontaires de grossesse par groupe d›âges de la
      femme, 2015
      (www.insee.fr/fr/statistiques/2851519?som-
      maire=2851587)
      Guttmacher Institute, Induced Abortion in the
      United States, October 2017

(www.guttmacher.org/fact-sheet/induced-abortion-united-states)

CDC, Abortion Surveillance - United States, 2014 (www.cdc.gov/reproductivehealth/data_stats/abortion.htm)

Region / Country	Region /Country Code	Nr Births per year(thousands)	Nr Abortions per year(thousands)	Fertility rate	Abortion rate
World	900	140,269	55,900	2.52	1.00
Africa	903	40,234	8,200	4.72	0.96
Asia	935	76,129	35,500	2.20	1.03
Europe	908	7,997	4,300	1.60	0.86
Latin America & Caribbean	904	10,929	6,500	2.14	1.27
Northern America	905	4,325	1,200	1.85	0.51
Oceania	909	654	100	2.41	0.37

France (source: Insee)	250	773	223	1.98	0.57
USA (source: CDC)	840	3,940	653	1.88	0.31

USA (source: Guttmacher)	840	3,940	926	1.88	0.44

Europe & North America		12,322	5,500	1.72	0.77

41   World Health Organization, Unsafe Abortion - Global and regional estimates of the incidence of unsafe abortion and associated mortality in 2008 (www.who.int/reproductivehealth/publications/unsafe_abortion/9789241501118/en/)

42   World Health Organization, Media Center, Pregnant Women must be Able to Access the Right Care at the Right Time, November 7, 2016 (www.who.int/mediacentre/news/releases/2016/antenatal-care-guidelines/en/)

43   The British Journal of Psychiatry, Abortion and mental health: quantitative synthesis and analysis of research published 1995-2009, August 2011, (http://bjp.rcpsych.org/content/199/3/180) US National Library of Medicine, Fatal Flaws in a recent meta-analysis on abortion and mental health (www.ncbi.nlm.nih.gov/pmc/articles/PMC3646711/)

44   United Nations, Economic and Social Affairs, 2016 Demographic Workbook (https://unstats.un.org/unsd/demographic-social/products/dyb/dybsets/2016.pdf)

World Estimated Population(2016)	Annual rate of Increase	Crude Birth Rate (‰)	Crude Death Rate (‰)
7,467 M	1.1	19	8

	Population Increase	Births	Deaths
Total per year	82 M	142 M	60 M
Total per day	225,032	388,693	163,660

45   OECD, General government spending (indicator) - 2015, (https://data.oecd.org/gga/general-govern-ment-spending.htm)

46   United Nations, World population prospects, Key Findings and Advance tables, 2015 revision (https://esa.un.org/unpd/wpp/Publications/Files/Key_Findings_WPP_2015.pdf)

47   United Nations, Data Booklet, World Fertility Patterns 2015 (www.un.org/en/development/desa/population/pub-lications/pdf/fertility/world-fertility-patterns-2015.pdf)

48   United Nations, World population prospects, Key Findings and Advance tables, 2015 revision

49   The World Bank, Population Density (People per sq. km of land area), (https://data.worldbank.org/indicator/EN.POP. DNST)

	Population (Billion)	Density
World (2015)	7.5	56.7
World - High scenario	14	106
World - "awfully pessimistic"	28	212

50   United Nations, Economic and Social Affairs, Population Division, World Population to 2300 (2004) <medium scenario> (www.un.org/esa/population/publications/lon-grange2/WorldPop2300final.pdf) Combined with: United Nations, The World at Six Billion, October 1999 United Nations, World population prospects, Key Findings and Advance tables, 2015 revision

51   US Centers for Disease Control and Prevention, Growth Charts (May 2000) (www.cdc.gov/growthcharts/data/set1clinical/ cj41c021.pdf)

52   Cambridge University Press, The Journal of Economic
       History, Charting the "Rise of the West" Manuscripts
       and Printed Books in Europe, A long-term perspective
       from the sixth through eighteenth centuries, from Eltjo
       Buringh and Jan Luiten Van Zanden, June 2009 (tables
       3 & 4, p44-45)
       (www.researchgate.net/publication/46544350_
       Charting_the_Rise_of_the_West_Manuscripts_and_
       Printed_Books_in_Europe_A_Long-Term_Perspective_
       from_the_Sixth_through_Eighteenth_Centuries)

Century or Years	Per capita consumption of manuscript books annually per million inhabitants(Western Europe)	Access to Books (people reading an average of one book per year in Western Europe)
6th	6.5	1 / 153,846
7th	5.3	1 / 188,679
8th	20.9	1 / 47,847
9th	88.1	1 / 11,351
10th	52.6	1 / 19,011
11th	70.2	1 / 14,245
12th	206.1	1 / 4,852
13th	330	1 / 3,030
14th	507.8	1 / 1,969
15th	929	1 / 1,076
1454-1500	3,100	1 / 323
1501-1550	17,500	1 / 57
1551-1650	29,100	1 / 34
1654-1700	40,600	1 / 25

1701-1750	66,700	1 / 15
1751-1800	122,400	1 / 8

53   The World Bank, Individuals using the Internet (% of population)
(https://data.worldbank.org/indicator/IT.NET.USER.ZS)

Year	Individuals using the internet (% of population)	Penetration rate
1993	0.25	1 / 394
1994	0.45	1 / 222
1995	0.78	1 / 128
1996	1.3	1 / 75
1997	2.1	1 / 49
1998	3.2	1 / 32
1999	4.7	1 / 21
2000	6.8	1 / 15
2001	8.1	1 / 12
2002	10.6	1 / 9.5
2003	12.3	1 / 8.1
2004	14.2	1 / 7.1
2005	15.8	1 / 6.3
2006	17.6	1 / 5.7
2007	20.5	1 / 4.9
2008	23.1	1 / 4.3
2009	25.5	1 / 3.9
2010	28.9	1/ 3.5
2011	31.3	1 / 3.2

54 Cisco Public Whitepaper, The Zettabyte Era: Trends and Analysis, June 2017 (table 1) (www.cisco.com/c/en/us/solutions/collateral/service-provider/visual-networking-index-vni/vni-hyper-connectivity-wp.pdf)

55 Internet System Consortium, ISC Internet Domain Survey (www.isc.org/network/survey/)

56 Roger Penrose, The Emperor's New Mind (Oxford University Press, 1989)

57 BBC News, Brexit : How Much of a Generation Gap Is There?, June 24, 2016 (www.bbc.com/news/magazine-36619342) BBC News, Us election 2016 : Trump Victory in Maps, December 1, 2016 (www.bbc.com/news/election-us-2016-37889032)

58 Samuel Ullman, Youth, Jane Manner, The Silver Treasury, Prose and Verse for Every Mood (Samuel French, 1934) (www.bartleby.com/73/2099.html)

59 CNN, Eight Times Russia Blocked a UN Security Council resolution on Syria, April 13, 2017 (https://edition.cnn.com/2017/04/13/middleeast/russia-unsc-syria-resolutions/index.html)

60 United Nations Documentation Research Guide,

Security Council - Veto List (http://research.un.org/
en/docs/sc/quick/veto)

61   Michel Devèze, Une Admirable Réforme
Administrative – La Grande Réformation des Forêts
Royales sous Colbert (1660-1680) (Ecole Nationale
des Eaux et Forêts, 1962),
(http://documents.irevues.inist.fr/
handle/2042/33607)

62   RFI, D-Day Veteran Remembers Sword Beach 70
years on, June 06, 2014
(http://en.rfi.fr/visiting-france/20140605-d-day-vet-
eran-remembers-sword-beach-70-years)
The Independent, The Other D-Day: France com-
memorates 'forgotten invasion', August 15, 2014
(www.independent.co.uk/news/world/europe/
the-other-d-day-france-commemorates-forgotten-in-
vasion-9672555.html)

63   The Times, Churchill Feared French Declaration of
War, November 01, 2013
(www.thetimes.co.uk/article/churchill-feared-french-
declaration-of-war-rlqdml22v3p)

64   United Nations, Sustainable Development Goals kick
off with start of new year, December 30, 2015
(www.un.org/sustainabledevelopment/blog/2015/12/
sustainable-development-goals-kick-off-with-start-of-
new-year/)

65 Karolinska Institutet, UN's eight millennium development goals: Both a success and a fiasco, July 15, 2016 (https://ki.se/en/research/uns-eight-millennium-development-goals-both-a-success-and-a-fiasco)

66 Stockholm International Peace Research Institute, World Military Spending, Increases in the USA and Europe, Decreases in Oil-Exporting Countries, April 42, 2017 (www.sipri.org/media/press-release/2017/world-military-spending-increases-usa-and-europe)

67 René Barjavel, La Faim du Tigre (Editions Denoël, 1966)

68 Jean-Dominique Bauby, Le Scaphandre et le Papillon (Laffont, 1997)

69 The New York Times, Mahalia Jackson and King's Improvisation, August 28, 2013 (www.nytimes.com/2013/08/28/opinion/mahalia-jackson-and-kings-rhetorical-improvisation.html)

70 Rainer Maria Rilke, Briefe an einen jungen Dichter (Insel, 1929)

71 Pierre Teilhard de Chardin, Le Phénomène Humain (Le Seuil, 1970)

Made in the USA
Middletown, DE
27 October 2018